FEEDING YOUR INNER MONSTER

FEEDING YOUR INNER MONSTER

TOUGH MIND FOR TOUGH TIMES

Dr. David Picone and John E. Hunt

iUniverse, Inc.
New York   Bloomington

Feeding Your Inner Monster

Tough Mind for Tough Times

iUniverse books may be ordered through booksellers or by contacting:

iUniverse
1663 Liberty Drive
Bloomington, IN 47403
www.iuniverse.com
1-800-Authors (1-800-288-4677)

ISBN: 978-1-4401-4203-1 (pbk)
ISBN: 978-1-4401-4205-5 (cloth)
ISBN: 978-1-4401-4204-8 (ebk)

Library of Congress Control Number: 978144014203

Printed in the United States of America

iUniverse rev. date: 5/28/2009

Prologue

Why We Wrote This Book

Many self-help/life guidance books revolve around one of several basic concepts.

The first is to define a widely desired goal and write a book on how you can reach that goal ("learn more," "earn more," "be more popular," etc.). The problem is that achieving a complex goal means completing a series of steps towards that goal, which seems obvious. However, because the steps are often unclear and new, it is difficult to define and link the steps.

Going to your local grocery store is a relatively straightforward process, as you have been there fifty times. Going to that exciting new shop, named Pencils or Extravagance, or something like that, somewhere on the other side of Manhattan, that your friend told you about at a party after a few drinks, is a lot tougher. Reaching a complex, real world goal is far closer to the Manhattan trip. Simply defining the steps towards the goal can be a huge problem. Conceptual goals are much harder to understand and define before you start than a trip to a store is. If you don't grasp the concept of the goal, your journey will not reach the result you wanted. If you finally reach the store in Manhattan, and discover that it really is a Goth clothing shop instead of the Celtic bookstore you anticipated, that's what happens when your goal hasn't been clearly defined.

Self-help books typically define the conceptual goal(s) and process in terms of various virtues—for example, persistence and/or cooperation and/or courage —which are meant to be shorthand for certain types of actions. The result is multiple virtues and/or vices thrown at the reader for 'guides'. The books are typically incomplete and/or incoherent regarding the interaction of the individual virtues/vices, to the extent they consider the interactions at all. It is more typical to simply assume the reader can balance all the unclear virtues/vices on their own. The actions flowing from the definitions are thus confusing and impossible to implement. This works well for the writer, because failure is your fault.

More importantly, by focusing on the social goals and definitions, the books ignore what you are and what you're capable of. The traditional books have a "fit in" and compress the self orientation, assuming that the greater social whole as it defines the good is correct. These books paper over your real self with these behaviors that are supposed to reach the social goals. So if you do manage to succeed as defined in those books, is the success what you really wanted, and what is the cost to yourself?

Secondly, many of the books are simply lists of useful behaviors when interacting with other people. Most of those behaviors assumed a fixed social environment, like America in the 1950's. We don't have that fixed environment anymore: three television channels and a defined conformity from age five through age sixty five. We are still on the upward part of the hockey stick curve in change (meaning that the rate of change is still increasing, not leveling off). Therefore, rules and suggestions based on the past are many times worse than useless—they are actually harmful. For example, anticipating a lifetime career in one area, perhaps with one employer, isn't going to be a good plan for today's world.

Another standard type is the "inspirational" approach. That is usually a variant of type one above, but it is typically focused on "meaning," life goals, life objectives, and so on. In this format, the authors provide various stories to inspire and guide people towards certain positive goals. The problem with this format, even more than the 'achieve wealth'/measurable real world goal books, is that the end concepts are extremely vague and often indefinable. Working with an indefinable concept may leave the reader with a warm feeling but little in the way of useful steps to take.

This book takes a radically different approach from those discussed above. We believe readers will be able to use our approach to take clear steps toward the goals they have defined for themselves.

Many of the problems that people have are rooted in the manipulation (by different parts of society) of general social values to confuse and mislead them. As society is comprised of many actors, without a checking mechanism as to the use of values by various groups, it is hardly surprising that values are routinely used outside their intended spheres.

For religious, ethical, historical, and command-and-control

reasons, many of our social values have so many barriers built around them that evaluating them is neither encouraged nor even possible. Thus any rogue with a nice suit and a good haircut can cheerfully use whatever combination of values he wants to get his way. Question his motives, and he makes clear you are a bad person for questioning the values he is asserting. Even worse, the person/structure using the values may mean well and thus be all the more insistent that no one question what they are pushing.

Some religious groups will be offended by this book, because it looks directly at many values that have religious roots or are part of the structure of the organized religion. The book says that people have to examine the values thrown at them, not simply take whatever the authority in front of them is pushing. The religious groups should look at themselves in the mirror and ask how they can be comfortable with the wholesale misuse and abuse of the values they espouse. Why don't these groups object to blatant abuse of what they hold sacred by so many groups in society?

Just as a recent example, the banking industry, using "good faith," "honor," and "trust" in its dealings with customers, has become predatory, ruthlessly raising interest rates knowing people will be ruined and extending credit to non-creditworthy individuals and selling the loans so someone else loses. Yet the authors see person after person in financial trouble solemnly saying that they are the kind of person who pays their debts, and will sacrifice to meet their obligations. What about the obligations of the banking system, which they blatantly ignored? This isn't to say that many of people's problems are rooted in unwise actions. But to a greater extent that people accept, we are setup to fail by the structure.

The book takes a radically different approach to life. The book says that much of "you" is socially forbidden, exiled to corners of yourself. Successfully completing elementary school guarantees that. As an adult, the effort and time dealing with these socially created monsters is too wearing and wasteful. As an adult, you have to bring those exiled parts back within yourself, utilizing all of your abilities and strengths. You then stop fighting yourself, and move forward with life.

Why We Are Qualified to Write This Book

Dr. David Picone has a Bachelor of Science (1980), from the University of Massachusetts, and a Doctorate of Osteopathic Medicine (1987), from Kirksville College of Osteopathic Medicine.

Dr. Picone performed his residency in Psychiatry at Michigan State University, Department of Psychiatry, and a residency in Internal Medicine at Michigan State University, Department of Internal Medicine.

He is a certified diplomat of the American Board of Osteopathic Psychiatry, and a fellow of the American Academy of Neuropsychiatry. He is a board member of the America College of Neuropsychiatarists.

Dave has been a practicing psychiatrist since 1989, working in a range of treatment environments. He has extensive experience with organic injury disability and dementia cases, in a variety of contexts. He has had years of experience working with various types of addiction situations. He continually works with the less medically serious but still personally overwhelming situations that turn people's lives upside down. Finding effective methods to help people suffering through what the medical literature defines as "temporary events" (even though they don't seem very temporary to those going through them) has been a focus of his. He is also an assistant clinical professor at Michigan State University Department of Psychiatry.

John E. Hunt has a BA from Michigan State University in Sociology (1972), a Juris Doctor from the University of Detroit (1975), an LLM (Masters in Law) in Taxation from Southern Methodist University (1983), an MBA in Materials/Logistics Management from Michigan State University (1992), and a Master's of Science in Building Construction Management from Michigan State University (1998). He went through the Building Construction program because of his interest in planning and project management.

He has been a Certified Public Accountant in Michigan since 1981 and a member of the Michigan Bar Association since 1975. He has earned the Project Management Professional certification, (Project Management Institute) and is a Certified Information Technology Professional (American Institute of CPAs).

John opened his own practice in 1984 and has worked with thousands of clients over the years. His primary focus is tax, estate planning, and business law issues. Although this may seem like an unusual background to write a book of this type, accounting actually involves as many applied psychology issues as technical ones. People talk to John about money, which they rarely talk to David about. In this society, it is common to hear a person on their cell phone droning on about personal events that you can't believe they are disclosing to everyone. But they don't talk about money—that is really private!

John has seen people mislead by advisors in many ways. The most common methods by which people are financially and otherwise mislead are based on the use of social values, applied outside their correct context. Because of the importance of the social values asserted, the application and relevance of the values are not questioned by people. People then drop their normal skepticism, hand over their money to invest, and walk out. When you walk into a financial advisor's office, you'll likely see nice suits, nice décor, and expensive-looking computers—it will look and feel right. You should picture them in pointed hats and stirring cauldrons, because financial advice is foretelling the future, a really, really hard thing to do.

CONTENTS

INTRODUCTION

The socially unwanted parts of yourself don't go away. They sit in corners, angry. Taught to fear them, taught not to look at them, we spend too much of our lives running from shadows.

> "A man cannot be comfortable without his own approval."
>
> —Mark Twain, 1835–1910

Tell yourself of the darkness within…

As you read these first lines, the darkness within that you imagine is far different from what you will know when you read the same line at the end of the book. At the end of the book, the darkness will be a comfortable darkness, a place of strength and growth, not a place to fear and avoid. The dark is a place of rest and repair, and you need the dark as much as the light.

> "Character is what you are in the dark."
>
> —Dwight L. Moody, 1837–1899

Life is like a puzzle, with no picture of the finished puzzle to works towards, with pieces seemingly unrelated and randomly handed out. Sometimes one doesn't even see the pieces as they are given. Can you put the puzzle together yourself for your life, or will you let others give you their solved puzzle, which meets their needs?

This book is an intellectual adventure, turning the normal way of thinking about things upside down. The *new* is impossible to understand before it occurs, so keep an open mind.

As you read it, things will strike you. Authors always want you to re-read their book, but we promise that things will pop out the second (and hopefully more) times you read this one. The book is both a reorientation of the way people relate to themselves, and a reevaluation of the virtues/vices that are used for command and control in society.

So, depending on your preference for visualizations, you will see through/break down a limit/wall to discover other limits/walls. The process of seeing yourself in a new way and changing the mental model used to evaluate choices will not happen in a day. You will grow like a tree, and like a tree, the strongest growth is slow. Oaks take longer than scrub, but they represent a greater accomplishment.

This is a book for adults, dealing with adult topics. Commonly, adult thinking is required when something awful has to be done. The adult thought advocated by this book is a completely different orientation from that type of adult thinking.

Conceptually, this book is an idea weapon, which should be used carefully by a competent operator. Adults evaluate choices and make decisions, while a child is told what to do. This book isn't idiot proof, because the world is more complex than that. Just as you would not own and use dangerous machinery without care, you have to think about what you are doing as you use the ideas in this book.

The glorification of children in society is partly a praise of innocence and lack of knowledge. Adults need knowledge, and you can't, by definition, revert to a state of innocence. Besides, the loss of innocence is generally expensive and painful; going through it once is enough.

Innocence is idealized by those who can't accept a difficult world. There are two groups who value such a lack of knowledge: those who would like to pretend that not knowing is the same as what they don't know doesn't exist; and those who are happier when others don't know what they are up to.

People who say that they love children's spontaneity, creativity, and excitement about life often spend their lives busily proceeding to crush out all of the above, because those attributes are difficult to control. The English way of resignation is much preferred by the established structure. This book wants to bring a child's spontaneity, creativity, and excitement back into adult life, with an adult perspective.

The goal of the book is to be a practical guide to handling life's situations. It is in overt opposition to many of the traditional self help books, which tend to be "go along" books. As discussed in the Prologue to the book, the usual advice/life book has a basic orientation towards compress yourself to fit; this book is focused on being yourself so you know where you want to go.

PART I: ESSENTIAL IDEAS

Chapter 1: Freedom

This book is about freedom. Real freedom is in your mind, knowing all of yourself. Freedom isn't something given to you; control by others is what is handed to you. Freedom isn't showing the front that society or the latest trends demand that you present.

Freedom is:

- Active peace: emotional calm, even in the tug of daily life

- Active meditation: visualizing yourself and growing, not disappearing into their void

- Choosing your friends based on what you care about, not what you should care about

- Enjoying social events and experiences because you wanted them, not because they were imposed

- Defining your choices based on what you want

- Not playing nice when you don't want to be

- Taking time for yourself, private and alone, when you need to think, feel, and grow

- The ability to raise your fists in your mind, against any person, institution, or social structure

- Acting as you think best, to focus and reach goals, to put aside nerves and scattered thought

- Being more than a wage slave, accepting your place in their hierarchy, drooling after the baubles that the advertisers throw in front of us

- Being more than climbing a social ladder to imitate people that you wouldn't have as friends if you knew them

- Using the resources and time you have in the way that you find important, satisfying, and enjoyable

You have to be tough inside to make it in this world. If you are willing and able to resist, to pursue your goals, and to understand what people are trying to do to you, then you are free.

> "The few are those who prepare against others. The many are those who make others prepare against them."[1]

Controlled and domesticated is the opposite of free. Freedom is knowing that you didn't learn everything that is important in kindergarten, and that overcoming the command and control devices drummed into you is part of gaining your freedom.

Inner freedom leads to outer freedom, as well as understanding. We all have corners of our mind that we avoid or don't peer into often. In reality, the courage required to think different things is greater than that required to do dangerous things. Doing dangerous things in a group may be the result of peer pressure (yes, if everyone else was jumping off the cliff, you would too). Thinking new and possibly dangerous thoughts—well, that takes place inside yourself, and you have to hold your own hand.

Freedom isn't:

- Defining yourself by how you fit into society, or, more importantly, defining yourself by how you defy social rules

- Being dependent on others' opinions and actions for your happiness

- Taking predefined bets as to how to run your life—anytime you take a predefined bet, you have already lost; it's just a matter of how much they figured in for you to get so you keep playing the game. So if you bet on red in roulette, they know the odds before they take the bet. Conceptual bets that society wants you to make have the same constraints, but are much harder to see.

---

[1] *Sun Tzu*, "The Solid and Empty," *The Art of War*

- "Renting" your emotional support system from another person or social structure, so that they have the final say on how you should feel about yourself

If you prefer goals and rules that are confusing and contradictory, unworkable and frustrating, then stay where you are. If you want to reach your potential as a complete individual, read on. Freedom isn't easily gained. Freeing yourself from years of contradictory and inconsistent rules and ideas doesn't happen overnight. You have to want to be free and keep that desire burning in your heart.

Chapter 2: The Good Is Them, the Bad Is You (Not)

Society isn't foolish: the rules are defined so society functions. There is no question that it is important that society functions. We are all worse off if each individual has to grow his own crops (and process those crops), perform surgery on himself to repair his insides, and build his own computers from sand he finds on the beach. It just can't be done.

Each individual is obviously bound into the greater social whole for the necessities and luxuries of life. Each of us exchanges his time and skills, to varying degrees, for those necessities and luxuries.

Which Is Most Important, Society or the Individual?

The critical trick is that society then defines the greater social whole as more important than the individual. Once that definition is accepted, then that greater social whole, which is really nothing more than someone or a small group pulling the levers, can run amok, pursing their goals regardless of the cost to the individuals in the group.

It is easy to see how this happens. Economic functioning is everything for a social group—you have to have food and security so there is a group tomorrow. Economic functioning requires people to do (a) certain things, at (b) certain times, and in (c) certain ways. Because those (a) things, (b) times, and (c) ways are not what people necessarily want to do, society has to demand that those things be done, and that demand is couched in terms of very real and vivid physical actions. So the actions have to be done.

There is an important distinction that has to be made before the assumption that the greater social whole is more important than the individual is accepted. The greater social whole is more important than the individual for the things that, if not done, result in no society and no individuals. For example, we must seed the ground at the right time. If we do not, everyone clearly loses. In a traditional agrarian society (early Egypt and the middle east) it took a carefully controlled group effort to plow the soil, control the irrigation flows, and other necessary steps.

But the greater social whole is not automatically more important than the individual regarding the multitude of actions and choices that are not critical to the continued economic existence of the society, but merely benefit some person or group. That is the jump that has to be rejected by the individual. If that jump isn't rejected, people suddenly have the three hundred greater and the three thousand lesser social rules provided in the Confucian system binding their every action and thought. As the military knows, discipline is critical, because if you keep people focused on the small stuff, they obey and don't think about the large stuff.

We are thinking about the large stuff. In this range of cases, at one end, we have the economic necessity to society, which trumps individual rights. At the other end, we have the will of powerful people, who impose their personal whims on others for reasons that either have nothing to do with the economic structure of society or actually damage that structure. The argument that society is more important than the individual must be rejected in the non-critical cases.

"V for Vendetta" argued that people should not be afraid of their government, and that governments should be afraid of their people. Governments like the blanket assumption that society is more important than the individual. When you decide that the individual is more important than society in certain (and there are many) situations, that scares the government.

All societies co-opt their various ethical, moral, and religious system(s) for command and control of the critical and the non-critical actions discussed above. Rewards and punishments are used equally on those actions that can destroy society, and those actions that discomfort the elect. Society makes the offer of the life to come dependent on society getting what it needs now.

This is distinct from the religious aspects of the life to come-what we are considering here is society's use of control mechanisms. Alternatives are resisted because of the walls and barriers built around the command-and-control positions. While each person has to take his/her own position on the life to come, each of us must understand what they give up to the command-and-control structure in the here and now.

In ancient and traditional agrarian societies, people did what they were told, with few choices. Physical skills were interchangeable and thus individuals expendable. In today's world, people have choices and opportunities, and they want to exercise them. Knowledge skills are not interchangeable and individuals with those skills are not expendable.

Society Needs the Individual

There is a chicken-and-egg aspect to the relationship between the social structure and the individual. Clearly each needs the other, and neither can exist without the other. The extremes in the relationships are marked on one side by slavery, where individuals have no rights, and at the other end by anarchy, where social structures are rejected for complete (theoretical) individual freedom.

Many societies have tried to avoid recognizing individual rights. Individuals are annoying, and trying to get them to do something is like herding cats. Traditional monarchies recognized only one person—the god/king/emperor, and all else were property. An ancient world example was Egypt. More recent examples were the Russian czars, and the Chinese emperors. While there were various status people could be in the society - nobles, warriors, farmers, merchants and serfs/peasants, for example - the King/Emperor had complete power, at least in theory.

True slavery, where a person is the chattel of another, meant that the slave had few, if any, legal rights and was just told what to do. Death was the alternative to obedience.

Today's world has multifaceted systems that assert ownership over the abilities of the members, but which are not called slavery. It is more fashionable, rather, to describe individuals as members of the social structure, using group structures such as socialism, fascism, and communism. Those systems exult the social entity above the individual, with the same crushing results to the individual members of the group as slavery.

There are several advantages to these new concepts. First, those systems present a more conceptually complex definition, so that a large portion of the population can't even understand the way their society works. Eventually people tumble to the fact that the commissars have a better life than the proletariat, but it takes some time.

Secondly, it means that even though the government/society can force individuals to work as hard as they can (from each according to their ability, to each according to their need) that society doesn't have to carry them economically if they stumble, because the continued existence of society is the critical reference. People who can't contribute to society, threaten the existence of the greater society, and so are not necessary. And for those who didn't toe the politically correct line (or had the right friends), they found the needs they presented to the government discounted in value.

Traditional slavery systems rarely killed people as soon as they were not economically useful, as it caused too much disruption with the rest of the slaves. As a result, they carried a certain number of economically non-productive people. The gulag didn't have those restrictions. If you were not producing your share, you were an enemy of society. Enemies of society fare poorly.

The net result is the same, whether there is clear legal ownership or implied social ownership. Humans don't do well as slaves. They die; they don't work. They don't bring themselves into the work—their creativity and abilities. Thus the abilities of the leaders drive the entire system. As the abilities of any leader are limited (some more than others) and the passive resistance of the individuals is an economic drag, the system eventually collapses.

The virtue of democracy is that it engages the individual abilities of the members of the group. Democracy harnesses those annoying characteristics of individuals to focus on their own good, and through the multitudes focusing on their own good, the greater social entity prospers. Property ownership is critical, because people lavish their intelligence, care, and effort on what is theirs. This stubbornness of individuals has caused considerable anguish to those who believe that "from each according to their abilities and to each according to their needs" is the righteous way, since that slogan just doesn't work. There is a funny saying: it's plausible, are you sure it isn't true? The problem arises when people make the jump from plausible to true because it just should be true.

Even though the overall concept seems proven—people do better minding their own interests than being told what to do—it isn't that easy. Societal deterioration and rot from the inside because of the oppression of individual rights occurs slowly. The advantages to power and control by a certain group are immediately apparent, at least to that group. So the fight for individual rights in society will always continue. The names for the concepts will change over time to trick the unwary, but the essential dynamics are constant. Tyrants are little changed from ancient times to today.

The Social Compact

Each individual surrenders some possible freedoms and choices for the functioning of the social entity, and the social entity, by its lights, surrenders some of its potential power to keep the individuals functioning. This is true in all countries. The United States, in theory a democracy that exults the individual, defines all income in the tax code as being owned by the State, which graciously allows the citizens to keep what the State doesn't want. Section 61 of the Internal Revenue Code provides that gross income includes all income from whatever source derived, unless specifically excluded by law.

The social entity has very clear limits to what external actions it will accept. There are organized and armed entities out there to control external behavior in all societies. The problem with any tool, which is what a group of armed and obedient people can be considered, is that if a tool exists, it will be used for different purposes than for originally intended.

If you have only a hammer, you will use it to drive screws and open bottles. While we all agree on the need for personal safety and property rights (even thieves and murderers are fussy about their stuff and their lives), society's armed group also enforces the questionably useful but emotionally important beliefs of the legislators/power structure. All of those laws structuring how people 'should' behave, that pile up like cordwood. And they accumulate: newspapers, on a slow news day, routinely have articles on inane/outmoded laws that are still enforced-often as felonies.

We are fortunate that we live in times where the views of this book, attacking the falsity of the social structures restraining an individual's thoughts, can be published. It is important, as discussed throughout the book, to carefully distinguish internalization from externalization. Most prohibited externalization (going out and do-ing something) is really a response within and defined by the social entity for command-and-control reasons. Are you fighting to impress another, and/or preserve your social standing? Are you drinking to show your passive dissatisfaction and disagreement with something you can't directly challenge? The goal of this book is to focus on your definition and thought, so you do not act just because or because not as the social system demands.

The "Good" Is Them

So the good, worldwide, is defined as what is good for society func-tioning, as perceived by the leaders and decision makers over time. Putting the teeth into that definition of 'good', society uses all levels of command and control available for enforcement. Legal, ethical, moral, and spiritual systems are all co-opted and hijacked where necessary to ensure compliance.

The sad thing about the system is that leaders and decision mak-ers have bought into the system so fully that they can't even see the parameters of what they are deciding, because they can't see outside the system. The system defines them, and so they can't look outside. So they simply ape the past, or rationalize their needs as necessary. Hypocrisy is derided, but is it far more dangerous when the leaders believe in the system without question, as they have nowhere to go if things stop working.

The good is following the rules. Fitting in, not making waves. The good is: teamwork where you do what you are told, when you are told, how you are told, and no asking why. You dress as you should, you pray as you should, and your role models follow those rules. So the selfless person at the school, or church, or neighborhood, who always has time and a smile, is the ideal. The person who drinks too much, well, they are part of the system also, because they are misbe-having as the system wants. Society needs models and object lessons, as long as they function within to the system.

The person who asks questions, smiles at the wrong things, and thinks about the rules and why, they are not the good.

9

The good is what elementary school teaches: do your homework, sit quietly, play when and as told, listen and do not talk, be malleable and not difficult. Practically, those behaviors are necessary to some extent when you have a group of people that have to work together. The mistake happens when we extol those behaviors as absolute virtues, past the practical need to minimize frictions within the group.

Society Does Not Honor Good Faith

The enforcement of the "good" occurs at several levels. First, there are the armed groups, who you don't want to engage.

This book's concern is the enforcement that takes place in the space between your ears. Society spends a great deal of time and effort setting up the thought police inside each of us. Some of the rules are absolutely necessary for the group to function. But there are so many levels of nonsense piled in over time, as a person grows through different stages, that the rules become contradictory and incoherent. The thought policeperson says 'no' to everything, including thinking about why. Trying to evaluate all that conflicting stuff, with the usual tools and approach, is almost impossible.

Very importantly, there is the issue of good faith. Good faith is social glue—we act in a certain way because we believe the others involved and/or society, will act in a certain way for certain reasons. In short, we are saying, "We are doing this for you and you are doing this for me," with the intent that both parties will be better off.

The concept of and need for good faith may be hardwired into us. Dogs, for example, who shake hands without receiving a treat, but who then watch other dogs treated for shaking hands, will become surly and not want to shake hands.

Society, many times, does not practice good faith. This is not a value judgment; it is just a fact. Many parts of the system are designed to deliberately trick and confuse you. Confused people need guidance, which is what the system likes. Uncertain people freeze, and frozen people are passive and one less problem for society. Confusion and uncertainty can be profitable for a wide number of service providers.

Society, comprised of many actors, doesn't have a checking mechanism, and so segments can cheerfully distort broader social virtues to their own ends. Words, fitting into a pattern that means something in a language, may refer to nothing that actually exists. People believing that the words can make the reality is a profitable game for those pitching, but a losing game for those trying to hit.

For example, a classic stock fraud is to mail out a suggested stock pick to a large number of individuals, with one half of the mailings receiving the suggestion to buy, and the other half receiving the suggestion to sell. The half who received the suggestion that made money will receive another mailing, again one half buy and one half sell. Eventually, there will be a core of people who received four mailings that had the right advice, and those people are called about the fifth stock suggestion. They are sold a stock that the broker makes a lot of money on. Actually, the broker had no idea about what would go up and down, and the 'findings' that the mailing was correct four times in a row was just words arranged to represent something that didn't happen.

So if you assume that society wants you to grow, succeed, and become what you can be, you are incorrect. If you want to grow, succeed, and become what you can be, you need to understand where you are being tricked and how to see past these tricks.

While this may sound like paranoia, moderately bad economic times are actually the best for the power structure. People don't question, they are focused on survival, employers have more potential employees to choose from, and they work harder. This is not to say they want it that way, but keep it in mind the next time a sacrifice is called for.

The "Bad" Is You

So, the bad is then you. Not doing what you are told, doing what you want. Doing things when you want, not when you are told to. Questioning what you are told. Treating life like as experience for yourself, not merely as a production element.

The Bad is defining what is important to you, not just picking from choices (a), (b), and (c). The Bad is sleeping in, not being where you should be when you should be. You are organic: your body is an embarrassment; it smells, demands attention and time, and generates feelings that are hard to ignore. You disrupt social behavior and the system through your foolish self. Worse yet if you are female, since you can throw the entire village into a riot.

And what if you no longer want to be the 'bad'?

The critical difference today is that the economic times allow for more freedom and choices than we had in the past. Defining the greater social whole as more important than the individual was simple in the past. With an agrarian economic structure, this was probably true. Work was straightforward, bodies were interchangeable for the work, and it took a group to get that harvest in. No harvest, no group. The death of a few to admonish the rest was probably a net economic gain because it meant there were fewer mouths to feed.

Today, it is knowledge work that matters. Any work beyond digging a hole with a shovel takes knowledge and judgment. Knowledge work takes thought and ability, which cannot be forced. Individuals with skills are not interchangeable parts. If you are one of those individuals, you deny yourself by not looking around and seeing that things don't have to be the way they were fed to you. The society denies itself by losing those critical abilities of thought and skill.

Why it is absolutely critical that the individual stops being the 'bad'.

The times are calling for very difficult changes and different thought patterns. We have made a winner-take-all bet on technology to solve all our problems. It is very serious: humans are a monoculture, and monocultures attract parasites like moths to a flame. Past epidemics are proof of this. Human society is based on a very few monocultures: wheat, rice, corn, and fish. A parasite seriously damaging any of those monocultures means a lot less people in a short time. The oceans are rapidly being fished out. The end game in an exhaustion of resources scenario, using a 'tragedy of the common's' analysis, is often sudden and extreme.

Human beings have several critical systems keeping them alive: respiratory, digestive, etc.-between seven and nine systems, depending on classifications. Human's typically die when after a number of years, something happens to knock one system out of kilter. The medical system fixes that system, but knocks two more out, which they patch, knocking three more out of whack, and so on to the end.

The economic system has multiple systems, which can be knocked out of kilter just like a human's body. The process of increasing food yields increases nitrogen runoff, which damages the oceans, for example, and there are many, many other examples. A quick extrapolation of current trends points to little oil, few fish, and a lot of other critical shortages in a relatively short time.

Given the number of humans and each of our daily requirements, we need new solutions to avoid dropping into another dark age as the resources vanish. Technological progress depends on individual ideas, and those can't be forced. The command-and-control devices of the past, focused on the group, will just drive us off a cliff.

The complexity of the world economic system, the exponential increase in knowledge, the possibilities of biological and computer science, both in the short and long term, make this world so different from traditional agrarian society that it is as though we live in a science fiction novel. But you don't want to be a bit actor, mouthing lines in that novel. You want to define your own part, making up your own lines.

Inner Monsters

Because you are the "bad," you shove all that bad away, and it becomes your inner monster. The dark, forbidden to feel or look at, is demonized when it pops up. Unfortunately, the "bad "is a very important part of what "you," are. Those parts of you that society sees as interfering with your use as an economic tool are critically important to you. By bringing out and embracing the "you," the inner monster, you regain touch with the forbidden parts, the "you" that you've pushed aside.

Simply stated, your inner monster is the part of you that society doesn't want to exist because it doesn't need that part. But you need all of yourself, and your inner monster is the method to finding yourself. You need all your abilities working for you, not lined up against each other, freezing your thought and choices. So there is method in this madness, this "jump to the left and then a jump to the right" from societies formal dance.

Why it is critical to be in touch with your inner monster? It is because of some rather interesting psychological defense mechanisms we all have. For example, there is *acting out*, the direct expression of an unconscious wish or impulse to avoid being conscious of the emotion that accompanies it. Acting out can be extremely damaging, because you suddenly do things that are contrary to what your official face has been saying. Acting out, by just following the motions of a poorly understood morality play, is one of the most dangerous things any person can do.

Reaction formation is your behavior, your official face, which is completely the opposite of what you really want or feel. Reaction formation is very dangerous, because it will work in the short term but not in the long term. By the time your inner, actual self says NO, you are well down the road and locked into something that you have been acting like you wanted very much. The difficulty is that by the time it hits, the steps taken to support the official self make it far harder to find the real self.

Dissociation is the temporary and drastic modification of one's personal identity or character to avoid emotional distress. Like reaction formation, you can go a fair distance with this before it doesn't work anymore, which puts a person truly up a creek without a paddle. Dissociation is a classic device in horror movies, where the packaged person steps aside and something else, unknown to all, steps out. Dissociation is what happens on the third date with that nice person you met at the bar.

If you don't recognize your inner needs, you will do something amazingly stupid, and probably more than once. The unaccepted inner self will externalize those needs without thought or understanding, and it will be as much a surprise to you as to the people you know. You will rapidly fall into the traps that society sets.

How many politicians, religious leaders, generally important people, and people you know each day do amazingly stupid things that negate everything they seemed to stand for, or everything they had been trying to build? One hesitates to include celebrities, as we are assuming thought processes here, but if they didn't do stupid things how would the pulp magazines survive? These actions happen because people can only ignore their inner self for so long; then the inner self just acts.

Your "self," the complete you, needs your inner monster (IM). Your IM brings in your strengths, your internal power that keeps you focused on what you need, not what someone thinks you should need. You stop fighting with yourself, you stop dreading the shadows we are taught to fear. Your IM keeps you in touch with yourself so you know what you are feeling and can see what you want to be doing, so you know where the conflicts are in your life. You don't want surprises or sudden eruptions. You want to plan, to make your life work.

CHAPTER 3: READING THIS BOOK

The uniform response by readers/reviewers and editors has been that the book discusses many ideas in Chapters 1 to 13, but that the ideas are not tied together from chapter to chapter. As a result, it can be confusing and unclear up to chapter 14, which is the dividing point in the book. From chapter 14 on, the consistent response is that it is exciting and takes a life of its own. So why not ditch the first part of the book, and elaborate on the last half?

The problem is that the last half of the book is built on the foundation laid in the first half of the book. If you have ever been involved with a construction project, you know that it starts with the clearing of the site, and the demolition of any structures on the site. Frantic activity is then interposed with periods of inactivity, when it seems like nothing is getting done. As time goes by, it seems like random holes and ditches are being dug, footings laid in the mud and an array of supports and walls laid out. Until the foundation is completed, and the carpenters start throwing up the outer walls, the building doesn't look like much, and it is hard to picture where we are going to end up. In real life, the foundation phase is a bad time to bring the bank officer in charge of the construction loan to the site, as they stare over the muddy mess with a distinct lack of enthusiasm.

The first part of the book, because it is the clearing/foundation process, focuses on an idea or set of ideas, explore that ideas(s), and then move to another set of ideas. The fusion and goal of the ideas occurs in Part III.

In writing, one can either (1) present the end result, and then retrace the process of reaching the end goal; or (2) slog through the process from beginning to end. We elected to slog from beginning to end. The authors would like to think that the first half is written with wit and polish, so that you can enjoy it, even though it is a little unclear (many would say very unclear) in parts. You can certainly skip to chapter 14 if you wish, and then go back to the first half if you like. We think that would ultimately be more confusing, but it is your choice.

As you read through the first chapters, and especially in part II, you will find at times it is unclear where the discussion is going.

Some of the chapters are demolition of existing structures, and some of them are building the foundation. The use of the various parts of the foundation being created is clear as you read into the second half, so please bear with us. The concepts and ideas discussed in the first half have had thousands of pages written about them. Picking from those ideas and writings what is needed for this book, and distilling those ideas down to less than a hundred pages, is going to leave a considerable amount of the prior literature unaddressed.

A related response from readers is that the foundation building deals with complex concepts, and there are not enough examples. To some extent, that was deliberate. Simply reading an idea and an accompanying example isn't nearly as useful as reading the idea and thinking through your own example(s). This book questions and challenges many of the basic assumptions we are taught about the relationship of the individual to him/herself and society. The book poses a complex, many layered analysis of and to revisions to those relationships. Each person is going to approach their relationship to him/herself and to society from a unique perspective. Only you can take these ideas into your unique thought and work with them for yourself, so the creation of your examples for yourself is essential. This is not a book with a pat set of steps to be taken in all situations and circumstances.

One emphasis of this book is on systems thinking: working through a system from the system's perspective. This is inherently frustrating, because when any of us decides that we want something, we want to move directly to the goal. We all become frustrated with having to divert our attention from the goal to learn a system to reach our goal—we just want to reach the goal.

Buying new computer software to accomplish a task is a clear example of the system problem. We buy the software to accomplish a task, and we know what we want accomplished, but if you force the software to reach the goal in the way you think if should be done, many times the software sabotages you. And by forcing the software, you don't learn the parts of the software that can do the job better, which is probably why you bought the software in first place.

So the book seeks to encourage you to think about the way

you look at things and how you think about things. Change can be demanding and frustrating, but not changing is worse.

As a side issue, systems thinking shows why losing weight is so hard. We want to be thin, which is a time delayed result of the interaction of a number of choices. Skipping food today won't help, because you will be tired and weak tomorrow and eat more. Exercising today will help, a little, but it is the continued set of actions: a little less food, and little more exercise, day after day, that lets you reach the goal. If you create and work within a system, you reach the daily goals, and the small, defined, regular actions reach the big goal.

As you read the book, you will see something, and look at it differently. An idea you had been mulling over becomes clear. Later, you will see something (and probably many things) differently, based on that first change of viewpoint. That continuing change of view doesn't stop; the authors are continually discovering new ideas and viewpoints based on the material in book. Many of the questions and issues examined do not have final answers in all situations. Situations change, and the answers and approach changes. 'Certainly' isn't possible, and the book does not pretend that it is. The book raises questions about the social glue we are embedded in, and how to choose future actions, and there can be no certain answers to the future.

Chapter 4: Key Ideas

Key ideas are the first level of foundation preparation. These are ideas that are so basic to the framework we use in looking at the world that we don't even think about them. But without pulling them out to examine them, we cannot get past the walls they build around us.

Key ideas can either be covered the first time they pop up or presented in one place. Both methods have advantages and disadvantages. In this chapter we present five important ideas. It seems more functional to us to put them in one place, as they are central to much of the book. Complete books have been written about parts and subparts of these ideas, so this discussion necessarily does not cover all points. The problem with 'making a long story short' is that everyone has different ideas about what can be omitted without missing the key issues. We ask the readers indulgence as we focus on what is key for the purposes of this book.

The Mean or the Ideal

This is a critical distinction that is glossed over in most discussions. The mean is a choice within a range of possible choices. Selecting a mean requires one to analyze and balance the various choices and possibilities, under conditions of incomplete knowledge and an unknown future. That choice requires thought and the acceptance of some ambiguity, neither of which are necessarily pleasant. An ideal, in comparison, is the goal to be reached. It is typically clear, and anything less than the ideal is inadequate by definition. So there is no thought about the choices, as the ideal is defined, and no ambiguity, as the ideal is the choice. Therefore, working with an ideal is much easier than using a mean.

Of course, there are many ideals, and they conflict. Pick the correct ideal for your purposes, however, and you can brush aside the rest. You are focused; you are clear. Whether you make any sense or not is another issue, but the internal compass is at least set. On the other hand, with a mean, there is always reanalysis and thought, and while what you are doing may make a lot of sense, your internal compass may be spinning wildly.

The reason the difference is so important is that in any choices you make, whether by yourself or in a group, you win your argument before you start if the target group accepts your underlying definition of the problem as an ideal issue or a selection of the best mean.

For example, if you define "X" as the only permissible option, there can't be any argument about whether the goal is achievable or not, or whether lesser measures would accomplish the goal. There can't be any argument about the effect on other goals—such as whether "X" is correctly measured, or has different aspects in different situations that the definition. You have won your point by a definition that wasn't even discussed, but which shaped and created the end points before the discussion began. The only real discussion available concerns the speed and severity of the steps involved to reach that goal. A focus on the ideal allows one to do anything to reach that ideal, regardless of the cost borne by others.

The absolute ideal of "X" is much easier to argue and pursue than the weighing of effects of "X" interacting with other social goals and issues. First, the clarity of the ideal makes it easy for people to focus on that goal. We all have limited ability to mentally juggle multiple topics, and so clarity of focus is mentally easier. Secondly, if you weigh multiple issues and topics, then not only does one have to face reality, but to then make choices about the future based on guesses and other's value ratings of those guesses. The questions do not have to be raised, if your goal is an ideal. Ideals have a satisfying certainty to them.

A debate defined by ideals really isn't a debate because there isn't any communication between the parties. Anytime the end point is defined as an ideal, there really can't be any discussion as the definition of the ideal.

Aristotle and Plato presented the two primary positions a very long time ago, and the argument had probably been going on for a long time before their writings. Aristotle said:

> "And so we may say generally that a master in any art
> avoids what is too much and what is too little, and

seeks for the mean and chooses it—not the absolute but the relative mean."[2]

The other side is presented by Plato, whose position was as follows:

"The goal of intellectual inquiry is to discover the eternal immutable forms of 'ideas,' which serve as the essence and ideal of all things; in this way a true philosopher seeks wisdom."[3]

The idea then becomes an ideal, and then is then applied to a goal by seeking that absolute ideal, as anything less, even though we live in a non-ideal world, would disserve the goal/group and/or point to be made.

The trick is to be aware of the ideal underlying the argument. If no one catches the ideal underpinning the argument, it's just a matter of time before victory. If the opposition does raise the underlying framework, then tying this ideal to another ideal or position that cannot be attacked solves that problem.

The reason we raise this early in the book is that society, and all of us, are very good at using absolutes to gain an advantage and win our discussions. This happens more and more in the modern world, as the vast amount of information spewed at us limits our ability to look past the words and images we are being bombarded with. This is important, because compromise is impossible where discussions are framed in terms of ideals. Compromise, being the art of the possible, keeps systems running, and failure to compromise competing positions effectively freezes the system. This applies to your internal system as well as any other.

All the virtues and other rules we examine later are typically presented in terms of ideals. Using them as ideals makes compliance absolutely impossible, as the ideals contradict each other. Your mind churns uselessly, trying to reconcile the irreconcilable. The only

---

[2] Aristotle, The Doctrine of the Mean, Nicomachean Ethics 11.6-7, http://www.wsu.edu/~dee/GREECE/MEAN.HTM

[3] http://www.philosophyprofessor.com/philosophers/plato.php

solution is to step back, recognize the trick in the definitions, and redefine the discussion.

Ideals are commonly praised and presented as goals. In reality, ideals are dangerous and need to be exposed in our thinking and the thinking of others. "Should be" has to be questioned, because there is always more freight behind that ideal than what shows on surface.

As an aside, when thinking about quotations from Plato and the other great writers, one has to remember that some of the language on the page represents the position of the writer. Some of the language represents positions that the writer had to endorse in order for society to accept the writings. Some of the language represents positions that were absolutely required to be accepted, lest serious harm come to the writer. And finally, where documents have been translated and re-translated over the centuries, into different languages and for different needs, words and phrases were chosen that may not represent the position of the writer. The net result is very close to the following saying: "I know you think you understand what I said; what you don't understand is that what I said is not what I meant."

Structure versus Individual

Structure is used here in the sense of a social, non-physical structure. Social structures are everywhere and include formal social structures and informal structures. Formal structures are governments, institutionalized religions, corporations and business entities, and many others. Informal structures are the group of people you meet at the bar and the people you talk to in the park when taking the children to play. In between formal and informal structures are semi-permanent structures such as church study groups and bowling teams at your favorite bar.

Chapter 2 discussed how society defines itself as more important than the individual. Each of those social structures does the same, to some extent. One of the maddening things about modern office work is that if you are not talking to someone, it is assumed you are not doing anything important, and so people want to talk to you.

Reading is the same: you're only reading, so let's talk. It happens so often and in so many contexts that people don't even realize it. So, that request from the church group to meet this Tuesday, or the notice from the bowling team making you treasurer, or the PTA setting up work schedules for the parents with minimal notice, well, these have to be done, because they are important to the group. What you are doing for yourself is subordinate to the needs of whatever group wanders along.

You have to stand up for your rights as an individual; no one else is going to. You have to think and decline when people ask you to do things you don't want to do, or which conflict with things you had already planned. You are important, and your plans are important. Your cat isn't depressed because it's just a cat and not a lion. It's happy being a cat, although more tuna would be appreciated. You should feel at least as valuable as a person, but moderate the tuna.

Religion: Spiritual versus Structural

Religion is both an individual spiritual exploration and a social structure. The spiritual exploration is something each person must do for him or herself. However, the religious part of the social structure is co-opted into a command-and-control device, regardless of the society.

People naturally feel tension when it comes to religion. On the one hand, the spiritual life offers peace, coherence, and meaning. On the other, the structure can take control of your life, over things that really don't seem to be the business of religion but are important for command-and-control purposes.

Religions do not start out as structures. They begin with a flash of understanding, experience, and belief by the visionaries. Then the structure gradually accrues, like barnacles on a ship, until the structure is frozen, separate from the experience and the belief. The jump from "right for me" to "right to control others" divorces the structure from the people, but the people still need the core of meaning that the religious structure presents. Someday we will find the part of our brain's wiring that drives our need to control others.

This book does not address or offer opinions on the ultimate truths of a particular religion or set of religious beliefs. The focus is on the uses and misuses of social values and markers in this world, which are almost constantly tied to and buttressed by religious doctrine. That misuse and abuse of values occurs in all cultures and countries.

However, by looking directly at values which are freighted with religious overtones, the book is going to upset people. There isn't any help for that, and a certain amount of upset can be helpful to force thought.

Whether you are at one extreme completely focused on spiritual communion with the creator as you perceive it, at the other extreme not interested in the issue, or somewhere in between, which is where most of us live, this book is equally relevant to your concerns. This book is concerned with the misuse and manipulation of values and rules in the here and now, in the corporeal and impure world that we live in.

Modern physics' most elaborate creation, string theory, the explanation for everything, doesn't even have math that works. Clearly, a universe that explodes from literally nothing for no reason to expand infinitely by unknown causes can seem like an emotionally unsatisfying concept. Each person has to search for him/herself for the cause of it all.

The prevailing scientific cosmological calculations indicate that what we perceive as reality—you, the drink in your hand, the Earth, the visible universe—constitutes such a small amount of the total stuff constituting the universe that we are almost a rounding error to the amount of dark matter and dark energy that is out there (and the precise nature of both of these is unknown).

So in about five hundred years, we have gone from believing that humans are the center of the universe to the knowledge that the universe we perceive is nothing but a marginal part of the actual universe. On the bright side, we suppose it's impossible for us to get any less significant. From a practical perspective, who cares? We have the daily life in front of us to live. But it is the nature of people to think about the edges.

Religion seeks the essence, and each person has to take that trip for him/herself. However, while taking that trip, you have to live on this earth and understand what is going on, or you will sin without even knowing it.

Suits in Rooms and Decision Making

The modern world is full of laws, regulations, and the like to protect us, or at least meet socially defined goals. What people don't realize are the huge limitations on possible outcomes caused by the basic structure.

The bureaucracy consists of people in a formal structure making decisions—suits at desks making choices about our lives. This structure underlies all formal decision making, and the steps leading to the decision making. Whether it is the College of Cardinals, the Senate, or all the myriad lesser organizations, there is a limiting structure that has to be considered.

The problem is that the formal structure doesn't allow a lot of feedback and information into the process. Only certain types of events are captured, and not all those events are considered (for good and not-so-good reasons). The underlying frustration with the "suits" system is that where the events to be measured are outside the "suits at desks" view, those events don't exist even if they are the most relevant facts. Getting a traffic ticket for going with the flow of traffic is going to be an enforceable ticket, even in the situation where going slower would be more dangerous. The nuances of events, which shape our choices, don't reduce easily to the 'objective' standards of allowed evidence.

The legal process is particularly formal, even more so than administrative agencies. This is good in many ways, because flexibility tends to go to the well connected, but it is another reason that things just don't seem to work. While in theory a considered, structured process eliminates discretion and favors, sadly it doesn't work that way.

Max Weber (the father of modern Sociology) believed that the invention of the bureaucracy was a watershed event for human society, because the process would decrease discretion. While having a bureaucracy structures decisions, and prevents some of the problems with discretion, as time went by more and more decisions and choices were allocated to the bureaucracy. As it turns out, bureaucracy it only multiplied the possibilities for discretionary actions by the government.

For example, in your town, the city sets speed limits on roads to make them safer. One day, when they are short of money, they realize that ticket revenue is a wonderful hidden tax increase on the "evil" people. The roads suddenly turn into speed traps to maximize public revenue, defended, of course, by layers of "good intentions." Best of all, it is a trap on tourists, since the locals know about and avoid the traps. Whatever can be demonized can be forced to pay the freight for other things. Try going into court to say that the speed limit for a given street is in violation of the standard highway safety guidelines and is actually a cause of accidents. You will be lucky if you don't get a fine for contempt and for wasting the court's time.

You Can't Explain or Know Yourself in Words

Please bear with the following discussion, which doesn't have enough pictures with it. We think it makes an important point, but it isn't something we usually think about.

Language is one of the most remarkable human abilities. It is the basis for the accumulation of knowledge. Accumulating knowledge about the external world is a process subject to experiment and verification. If a proposition is given, it can be tested. If the words describing the proposition are incorrect, incomplete, or inadequate, the definition and discussion can be corrected and supplemented over time.

Accumulating knowledge about internal events is much more difficult. The problem that traditional psychology has had is that the words can't be tied to firm definitions, and so they are of marginal use. Consider the word "sad":

What is "sad"?

What clusters of feelings are related to "sad"?

How deep is "sad" before it is "depressed"?

What difference does it make whether the person is four years old or forty, as sad must certainly change with time?

How much different is "sad" between a person whose dinner plans were cancelled and someone whose longtime friend died?

There are lots of adjectives and adverbs in all languages to supplement the description, but all the supplementary words have the same loose borders as the central words.

So when someone says he or she is "sad," you have a mental definition that is like a bucket of sand dumped on the ground. There is a central bulk, probably the heart of what the person means, but there are outlier grains spilling out all over, in all directions, any one of which could be what the person really means in their mind.

This discussion could go on for hundreds of pages, but the essence is this: without clear external objects for multiple people to view so they can agree on definitions, words can mean lots of things to different people.

Even solid external objects are difficult to define. The classic formulation of the problem of experience is the elephant touched in different places by three blind men. One feels the trunk and thinks an elephant is like a snake, the other feels the leg and thinks an elephant is like a tree, and the third feels the tail and thinks an elephant is like a bush. The point of the story is that people have to compare their experiences to build a complete model of the external object.

What the story doesn't say is that the actual opportunity to share knowledge is probably pretty small, because an annoyed elephant is going to make mash out of all three of the men fairly quickly. And that is a valid point, in that external objects rarely are in a state of complete stasis that they can be examined, and when they move out of a state of stasis, they are different objects. The combined definition of the elephant that the blind men create isn't of any use in predicting the behavior or actions of the elephant, which is probably the most critical thing we are concerned with.

All this discussion is headed towards the point that words and the logical structure they fit into, as social constructs, are not the same as the logical structures in your brain, which are physical in nature. So to describe your plans, goals, fears, and other internal objects in words requires a translation from your internal structure into that formal logical structure.

That translation is further adjusted by the whole baggage of words and correct structures, in that only certain things are allowed to be said in certain ways. This is getting far too close to German philosophy in wording and complete lack of clarity, so let's look at some simple examples.

In practical terms, only certain things can be said. Telling the judge that he is an idiot is extremely counterproductive, even if all of objective reality is on your side. Telling the tribal chief that you respect his authority as to the economically critical social functions, but you reserve the right to paint your hut a different color than he mandated, isn't going to go well either.

Bluntly, much of human conversation really isn't about conveying information. A very high proportion of human interaction is the equivalent to monkeys picking the fleas out of each other's coats: it is a kind of grooming or stroking that bonds the group together. This is absolutely important, but communication for those purposes has to be distinguished from actually trying to convey an idea.

You cannot trust words to convey to yourself what you are thinking and feeling. You are a coherent self, and a large part of the mind is wordless, whereas words and language are controlled by very specific parts of the brain. The other parts of the brain also work and provide information in their own way.

A concept like "sad" is crystal clear compared to the concept of "self." Self has had many books written about it, yet it is still truly murky. That is why in seeking what you want, you have to be open to other multiple avenues to gauge what you really want and feel. We all use our emotions, but they can be difficult to interpret because we are trained to limit what we feel or are allowed to feel. A useful resource is your gut, which never lies about it's opinion. Your "pictures" of things are also critically important (we hesitate to use the word "visions," as it carries a lot of freight). We are speaking here of the pictures from your dreams, pictures that flash in your mind, pictures as you lie between sleep and full wakefulness. In evaluating your choices, you have to consider how energetic you feel having made certain choices, the random thoughts that flash in as the day goes by, and how well you are sleeping. These are often subtle (at first, anyway) messages from the wordless mind to central. Ignore your gut long enough, and the messages stop being subtle.

Flowing from this problem with definitions is the logical manipulation of the word symbols. Logic only works if the words being used have meaningful definitions, as otherwise you simply have a structure that says nothing. Setting and achieving personal goals is difficult because the logical process we typically employ (which uses ambiguous words tied to inner emotional states) fails to take the entire system (including your non-verbal mind) into account. Thus the plans flowing from this "logic" will fail.

Chapter 5: Why Life Is Confusing

The reason for this chapter is that each of us is told that increasing our skills at the level we are at now will adequately prepare us for the future. That is partially true, but mechanically increasing a skill at one level doesn't necessarily increase your skills at the next level. In many cases, extreme competence at the level you are at will guarantee you will never rise, because you can't see what ability has to be given up, and new ones found, for the next level of life. As you grow and change, the skills required change, and one has to be aware of the enormous changes in skill sets required. We all have these skills, but we have to open ourselves to find the skills in us. Higher level skills are typically not developed in school or other training, because those skills are less controllable by society.

"No battle plan ever survives contact with the enemy."

—Field Marshall Helmuth Carl Bernard von Moltke,
1800–1891

What does this have to do with your inner monster? Looking at the changes that life requires helps us understand why so much of what we have been taught is worse than useless. Because things do change so much in life as we grow, knowing the differences at various stages, and remembering that the stages are there, helps us move on from where we are now.

The good news is that you probably already have the new skills you will need. However, you may have ignored them or even rejected them in the past, since you did not need them. Searching your mind for these skills isn't like searching a computer database (plug in the keywords and the skills don't pop out). You have to be open to your actual self for the abilities to come out.

Life's Requirements Change and Don't Tell You

One of the most interesting, but annoying things about life is that at every level in life, the next level requires skills that are at a ninety-degree change from what your present skills are now. There are two problems with this: One, perhaps your skills really are best suited for that CEO position in that large company (what you always thought); however, the in-between skills are blocking your rise. Two, the people who do rise probably don't have the right skills but rise past their level.

The Peter Principle says, "In a hierarchy, every employee tends to rise to his level of incompetence." This actually occurs because skills at the next level are completely different, not because the employee is incompetent. Competence and incompetence frames the discussion at the personal level, which really isn't correct. It makes an emotional issue out of an objective problem. Be like Toyota: the *kanban* system doesn't blame the person; it blames the system and changes the system. Likewise, don't blame yourself when the system doesn't work, although the system will be happy to blame you.

In traditional agrarian society, the roles were pretty simple, and the events outside the system—no rain, locusts, etc.—had more impact than the fact that the lord's son was an idiot. As long as someone could keep the irrigation ditches working and the seed in the ground, people ate. In today's world, the decisions in the system make much larger differences, and so a mismatch of skills is more dangerous.

An Example showing what Critical Skill Sets are needed at different Job/Work levels

A competent carpenter (physical and mental abilities) is promoted to group leader, where has to manage people, requiring completely different skills than a carpenter's physical abilities with tools. He is then promoted to project manager, where he has to schedule and plan. Successful there and eager for more, he then promotes himself, starting his own business as a builder, where has to sell, nurture credit relationships, and develop accounting and other business skills.

Things go well, and he becomes a larger builder, where the key skill is to delegate to people, who then delegate to the people down the road, who do the work. Choosing those people is a very difficult skill, as subordinates can be yes people, in which case you don't find out about problems until too late, or very competent, in which case

31

they leave to start their own business. Let's look at the example of Damocles:

> Damocles was an excessively flattering courtier in the court of Dionysius II of Syracuse, a fourth century BC tyrant of Syracuse. He exclaimed that, as a great man of power and authority, Dionysius was truly fortunate. Dionysius offered to switch places with him for a day, so he could taste first hand that fortune. In the evening a banquet was held, where Damocles very much enjoyed being waited upon like a king. Only at the end of the meal did he look up and notice a sharpened sword hanging by a single piece of horsehair directly above his head. Immediately, he lost all taste for the fine foods and beautiful boys and asked leave of the tyrant, saying he no longer wanted to be so fortunate. Dionysius had successfully conveyed a sense of the constant fear in which the great man lives.[4]

The ability to accept and function with that sword above your head is the driver for the risk you can take, and often determines how far you will rise in a social hierarchy. As a bigger builder, our one-time carpenter has to have the emotional ability to tolerate large risk exposures, and he has to deal with bankers. It sounds like fun being the leader until the emotional weight of having to carry all those people into unknown situations truly hits. Most of the money that CEOs of large companies are paid is for the ability and willingness to carry that weight.

In a famous story, Donald Trump was walking down the street with his girlfriend. It was 1991, a down year for New York real estate. Mr. Trump pointed to a man begging, and said, "He is worth $900,000,000 plus or minus, *more* than I am," which is what happens when leverage goes bad. He had the strength to endure (not a trivial matter), and the market turned dramatically in his favor.

---

[4] Wikipedia, "Damocles," http://en.wikipedia.org/wiki/Damocles.

To continue with the example, our friend (who is *not* the Donald) then becomes a *very* large builder. Now, political and financial skills—getting zoning, favorable treatment, large projects, financing, bonding—are critical, as well as the ability to interpret the advice he is getting from the professionals he hires.

The classic attorney joke:

Q: Why are medical laboratory researchers using attorneys instead of rats for experiments?

A: There are more attorneys than rats, the researchers don't form emotional relationships with the attorneys, and finally, there are things even rats won't do.

When dealing with professionals, you have to consider their advice carefully, as part of their advice relates to your problem and part of their advice is self-serving.

Finally, ultimate success comes to our friend, who becomes a *benefactor*. At the top of the social world, he is so rich that he gives money away, and he doesn't have to lower himself to making it. His days are spent interacting with all the others on the make, with occasional frantic dips back into the business to fire the idiot who almost drove it into the ground and get things on an even keel again. Oh, and avoiding the blondes who consider successful business people their natural prey.

The skills and mindset you need as you age are just as different, and require the same type of mental jumps. You are told what to do as a child, and the things you are told are not necessarily true (certainly only a small portion of the "truth"), but hopefully they will keep you alive long enough to grow up and learn other things. Part of the disillusionment that people have as they grow older is confronting that what they were told when younger was just wrong (or perhaps only partially true) from a mature perspective. We lie to our children, and should not be surprised that our parents lied to us.

Why You Can't Trust the People on Top

A key skill, perhaps *the* key skill, to rising to higher levels is the ability to bear the weight, to take the pressure and thrive on it. While people are flexible and can grow, this isn't a skill that can necessarily be taught. Part of the problem is that one never really knows about bearing the weight until it is loaded on. If you have ever stared at the ceiling in the night wondering where the mortgage payment is coming from, you have an idea of the parameters.

The key problem with choosing leaders is that the ability to bear the weight often is not correlated with the other necessary abilities—such as self-doubt, questioning systems—that would were the key factor's in Plato's wise man.

If you read European history, you'll know that it was fairly rare that a king was known as "Harold the Wise" and surprising how often a king was known as "Frederick the Foolish." But they were still kings, and had the power at that time. Your bad luck if your boss was Frederick.

So while we are often eager to hand off the load to someone who wants to carry it, their willingness to carry it has no guaranteed relationship to with our wants and needs when handing the power to them. That warm rush of emotion that follows putting your trust in another, and dropping your burden, isn't an acceptable criterion when making this choice.

The real danger of people carrying loads that they are emotionally but not mentally capable of carrying is that the ability of people to do evil in the name of good is essentially unlimited.

The last hundred years clearly demonstrates this. All the "bad" people—Hitler, Stalin, make your own list—had the weight of society behind them, and they were going after the "good." So when that aspiring leader walks up to you, pushing light, happiness, and a wonderful future for just a "little" sacrifice, step back carefully. We can recognize the guy pushing down the seventh whisky shot is on the wrong track, but those pushing the socially accepted markers can cause real damage down the line—and they have the armed groups behind them at that point.

Chapter 6: Modeling and Controlling Human Behavior

This chapter looks at several critical foundation issues. First, the mental model that we are trained to use creates walls that limit our possibilities. Secondly, the standard virtue/vice concepts as directions for living just don't work. That virtue/vice are not really useful as life guides is a direct attack on the command and control structure, and is a difficult mental step to take.

Why do we care about the model of human behavior when we are interested in our monster? Focusing on your inner monster is such a huge jump from the normal view that it's critical to understand where things went wrong.

What Is the Mental Model Used?

The prevailing mental model people are trained to use is that each person is a container filled with conflicting goals and desires in constant battle. The model says that there are different selves and issues that won't go away and can't be permanently resolved, only overcome by continual fighting and effort. The Freudian model, for example, has various subcomponents—the id, the ego, the super-ego—engaged in a battle all the time. The church uses angels and devils. There are lots of different approaches with different names and categories that war daily in the psychological profession.

Clearly, we are faced with differing needs in a day. We are comfortable asleep but have to get up—whether for work, feed the cat, or enjoy a nice day. We are hungry, but it's not the time or place to eat. We are lustful, but the rules are extensive when it comes to satisfying this desire. The truth captured by the existing model is that with the vast number of internalized rules, and the external ordinances, laws and regulations that we face each day, unless we can coherently organize those rules, there are different selves warring within us.

The argument of this chapter is that the model is incorrect, but created because it results in effective social control. Confused people are easy to sway. Unhappy people are easy to manipulate. Uncertain people "stay," like a trained dog. If the model says you are supposed to be conflicted, then you are stuck without their solution. So this model of humans as a package struggling with conflicting goals and battles needs to be reworked.

We don't need cheerful slogans ("Got hope?" "Be happy"); we just need to get out of our own way. Hope and drive is what your system produces automatically, just as you wake up in the morning. Happiness is a byproduct of doing what you should be doing, not what others believe you should be doing. There is hardly anything more completely self-destructive than throwing yourself into an obsessive desire to be "happy," as you then measure happiness by the momentary physical or mental results of actions (regardless of the consequences) and not by the feelings of satisfaction flowing from within.

We are not saying that there is a secret group of people who plan social control and devise the rules. As will become clear, those in positions of power are usually the most blind to the effects of the system, because they buy into it so completely. We all play the games ourselves when we get others to do what we want, but we don't step back to see the extent of the games.

Using an incorrect model can result in paying a terrible price. Look at all the people numbed and sedated through their day, whether through drugs (legal or not), food, alcohol, or other buy-offs. Recreational drug use is widespread throughout the world. If you have teenage children, you know that pretty much any drug is available at the high school – and probably the junior high school. It is so serious that the leaders of several major Latin American countries recently issued a report saying that the drug demand/drug war in the United States is destroying their countries.

Clearly people are medicating themselves for emotional/psychological reasons at considerable risk and cost. Lost potential is harder to track, but it is clearly there. Anger and frustration take a huge toll on daily life. The response of the system is to medicate further—don't step back and look at your life; keep on being an economic zombie.

As living beings, we are a reasonably functional set of physical systems and mental processes. Hearts beat, lungs breathe, feet walk—all astonishingly complex systems that function together, generally (and probably for the better) without our conscious thought. The body repairs itself, rests, and awakes revitalized, despite our best efforts to do as we think we should do, not what the body wants to do.

Many of a person's inner problems—demons you run from, in the typical formulation—could be considered as simply unfinished processes, as when you shut your computer down with the power switch instead of the system close. It leaves open files, possibly corrupts files, and causes general confusion. Perhaps you were too young when you became unable to deal with your events; perhaps the events were presented inside or justified by social markers that really didn't work. Everyone has these, and they continue to happen. Dented corners are just going to occur. What's essential is finding a method of dealing with them that *brings them into you*. All that energy going into avoiding the issues could be energy strengthening you instead.

Human Behavior: A Bundle of Sticks

The common-law legal system looks at real property law as a bundle of sticks. Sometimes all the sticks are used, sometimes only a few. They can be divided and recombined. A simple idea, but useful.

Human behavior is also like a bundle of sticks. There are a limited number of senses, and a limited number of physical actions from the various limbs and structures that can be combined into essentially infinite possibilities. The subparts of the brain, cobbled together from various evolutionary trees over time, have different potentials to deal with different situations. Perhaps the social (forebrain) brain deals with the complexity of social interactions, while the remnants of the reptile brain handle killing. Many of the possible sticks never need to be used, but they are there. Even if you have never seen a poisonous snake, your body will recoil if you see one (hopefully before it strikes). Monkeys do the same thing.

We are carefully trained, over time, to match certain sticks to certain circumstances. The rewards and punishments for our success or failure to match the correct sticks to the appropriate circumstance range from clear to impossible to evaluate.

A panda bear goes to a restaurant. He has lunch,

stands up, shoots the waitress, and walks out. The manager rushes after the bear.

"What are you doing!" he asks.

The panda bear hands the man a dictionary. Under the definition of panda bear's it says 'a large mannal from Western China that resembles a bear; eats, shoots and leaves.

So it isn't a good joke, but if you shoot people, the punishment is clear. What if you pick up a piece of trash from the street and put it into a wastebasket (not required by statute, no one watching, not your trash). What is the reward for that action? Why did you make that choice? You would have gained little, the decrease of a single piece of trash in the greater world?

If we look at our possible behaviors as sticks, then using the wrong stick (or using a stick in the wrong way) is a bad thing. We wasted time and effort ourselves, and whatever we hoped to accomplish didn't happen. Further, we may have incurred greater or lesser social sanctions, which may need additional actions, corrective actions, or other choices.

So we simply resolve to not do things wrong. Children quickly learn that doesn't work. What is a 'wrong' changes with time and circumstances. Knowing the results of an action before taking it can only be done if you have done the same thing over and over.

Unfortunately, "the only way to avoid mistakes is to gain experience. The only way to gain experience is to make mistakes." People don't usually realize that measuring the result of an action is actually enormously complex. Each action results in some kind of response, feedback, to that action. There is a huge range of possible responses to an action, most of which are ignored or not even perceived.

For little actions, such as eating a cookie, the result seems simple. Hungry, and then not. The relationship of the cookie to new, larger clothing, sugar in the blood, torn knees ligaments, and a range of other results—spreading out like ripples from a stone in a pond—is unknown and unknowable. You can't calculate everything; there isn't time. But just because you can't calculate everything doesn't mean that feedback isn't out there. Like your doctor, we operate on the heuristic that we look for horses, not zebras, and work with the common situation.

The danger is when the feedback points to a zebra but we refuse to see it. In the book *The Black Swan*,[5] Nassim Taleb argues that the improbable is going to happen, despite being defined out of our plans. Ignoring the zebra standing in front of you isn't going to work forever.

The behavior sticks have their appropriate uses. Like anything, used inappropriately, the stick causes harm. Some of the sticks are quite dangerous, which is why it is all the more important that you know your actual self before you choose to act.

Making Choices-Virtues/Vices Are Not Useful Guides

The prevailing model uses various internalized guides, learned over time, as rules to live by. Those guides are the various virtues and vices defined by the society we live in.

The problem with the virtues/vices as guides:

- They are good for society and bad for us.

- They are so unclear as to actions and measurable results that they are almost useless.

- They were defined and presented from historical situations and choices that are often not relevant to a present choice.

- They are phrased in religious and ethical terms that cannot be examined without violating very serious social rules, and thus questioning is off limits.

- They are picked up/learned haphazardly. What we learned at age four is grafted onto what we learn at age thirty, along with the movie character we liked and the bit from the book we read

[5] Nassim Taleb, *The Black Swan* (New York: Random House, 2007)

twenty years ago. There isn't conscious review and reconciliation of all of these pieces.

In short, they are coral reefs, built up slowly over time. Within the traditional world they were build around, they were walls to keep the wider world out. In today's world, where we must go to the wider world, the reef becomes a trap to tear the bottom out of your ship as you venture out to sea.

And you are thinking, "When is there time to review and organize all this information?" The answer is that we perform this review and reconciliation daily in our mind, but we don't listen to it. Things that are disagreeable, conflicting, and discordant are pushed into the dark parts of our mind, locked up so our official face (both to our social group and to ourselves) doesn't cause upset.

What the book will say, over and over, is that because the bad is defined as you—because of all this conflicting, incoherent "good" to adhere to—you need to find and feed your inner monster, to reach yourself and the coherence of yourself. Keep that concept in mind as you read this book.

It is easy to fall into traps where we stew and belabor the past—and sometimes this is fun. But that doesn't do any good. The past is done and over. It is pointless to be a victim. It doesn't matter what happened in the past; it is the future that matters. How many people have you known who had wonderful high school years and never really shook that world, so that their life is a refrain to what they did in eleventh grade? Is that really a life? We are looking at the next steps and what we are going to do now and tomorrow.

The number of books written on human psychology are legion. This short discussion of internal mental models is presented to focus on concepts that you can use. It is not a full proof or exposition for the priesthood of the profession to mull over. The priesthood has its own concerns and turf wars. Let's focus on ourselves.

PART II: WALLS AND BOUNDARIES

Chapter 7: You Are the Village Chief

While it would be fun to be the chief, why are we looking at that role when trying to find our inner monster? It is because we need to see what society wants out of people to understand why the rules and roles evolved as they did. Seeing what the rulers thought they needed out of their subjects is a critical step to knowing what can be dispensed with and what is absolutely critical.

In short, what kind of command and control structures would you create as chief so that the village functions as you want?

Imagine you are the chief of a small village—probably because you assisted the last chief in his transition to a different plane of existence. His vision for the tribe was outdated, and he didn't see that. You now have the nice hut, but now you need to keep the group going. You need food for the group; starving people are difficult to work with and may revolt, and most importantly, your family has to have food.

Thus, people have to plant, harvest, make clothing and weapons, clean, and get water, among other things. The people need reasons to stay in the group and obey you, and perhaps you need some rationalization for your ascent to power other than "I wanted it." You certainly need to provide a basis for your ascent to power deeper than "I could," because that works also for the next person interested in your job.

Someone has to work in the fields, which is backbreaking work.

Someone gets to tell people what to do, which can be done in the shade with a cool drink.

Someone has to create clothing, tools, and weapons, build housing. In a very small group, people do multiple roles, resulting in inefficiency. You have to adjust for the production limits and plan ahead.

There are very demanding needs from various groups: raising the young, keeping the workers healthy, healing the sick, carrying the aged, which, most importantly, includes older chiefs and warriors. The young don't carry their economic weight, but you have to have them for a future. The aged don't carry their economic weight, but they may have other skills, and they are people's parents and grandparents. Healing the sick, as well as making sure that the sick don't infect the entire group, is critical.

Someone also has to protect the group from enemies. While the warriors are often not the brightest, they tend to become chiefs, because they know how to use weapons. Someone has to minimize economic damage through theft, which usually will be the warriors, as they already have the weapons. Unfortunately they are probably the people doing the stealing, but making the outlaw the police has a long and honorable history.

In all the choices, there is a cost/benefit analysis that has to be performed. People will deny that some things—life, peace, whatever virtue or goal you want to raise—are not subject to the mechanical calculation of cost/benefit. But everything is. Whether it is a formal calculation, a back-of-mind doubt that is quickly pushed away, or something in between, the calculation has to be made. There are only so many resources, and there are absolute constraints to how they can be used. Everything takes some resources and creates constraints that affect other parts of the puzzle. The leader has to make those choices, and they are not easy or often pleasant.

Humans are large, dangerous animals, surly and difficult to control. If you have any doubts, remember junior high school or high school. If you have any doubts after that, go on a field trip to a prison or drive (carefully) through the less reputable parts of a major city. People just won't do what they are supposed to do. They get mad, followed by bad feelings that may result in killing. They get lustful, and there are more bad feelings, and then more mouths to feed. And our ancestors were much more violent and uncontrollable than we were. We are the survivors of those who got along. The people who stood out, the really uncontrollable people, were eliminated along the way.

The Romans were reputed to, when there was an uprising in the empire, to make a desert and call it peace. Twenty years later, when the city was rebuilt and a new generation grown up, they would do it again. That particular heavy-handed approach to control has thankfully been put aside in most of the modern world.

Above all else, from your viewpoint as chief, no one is allowed to whack the current chief. A clearly hierarchical religion with significant sanctions against rebellion is always put into use, along with a priesthood class. The Egyptian God/King pharaoh would be an example. Unfortunately, setting up a priest class means that they then define good/bad as rewards their group. Remember that important people in the village, especially those with weapons, continually review their options. It isn't personal, it's just business. You want them to remember that their happiness and social position depends on your continued existence.

From the point of view of the people, the minimum requirements usually include safety from theft, generally personal safety, (specifically no killing them or their families), food, and shelter. Also, male/female relationships mustn't tear the group apart. Fail as leader to provide those basics, and things will eventually crumble.

This, of course, assumes "good faith" on the part of the leader, i.e., that he cares if the system survives him.

> "Après moi, le deluge."
>
> —Louis XV

The leader doesn't always care if the system survives him. And the leader doesn't necessarily care that the system even exists outside him and his entourage. North Korea and some African nations are holdovers from the Age of Kings, in which the people were for the king.

Whether through divine intervention, painful experience, or thought and learning from other cultures, the village has devised some rules, which you internalized as you grew up in it. You, as leader, will continue to enforce some or all of those rules. You adopt those rules partly because they are "the rules," partly because the rest of the village can then buy into your position of power, and partly because at least the economic functions keep things going. As the new leader, you do have the opportunity for some fine tuning for your benefit, perhaps to benefit the group as you see fit.

If you, the reader, want to enrich your understanding of the village, and bring a lot of fantasy into your life, read the Conan the Barbarian novels, by Robert E. Howard. The books depict primitive systems of rules among many cultures. They are also a lot of fun to read, with the caveat that they are not in the least politically correct.

If you want something that is more politically correct, the Clan of the Cave Bear series is fun to read.

What complicates things is that people being what they are, you as the chief must buy into the rules, emotionally and intellectually. Hypocrisy, the deliberate presentation of falsity as truth, is an abhorred vice, so you don't enforce the rules without believing in them.

It is far more dangerous, but more common, to follow the virtue of truth (i.e., the rules are the right), since you can't think about what you are doing without jarring that certainty of purpose. So if you as chief see the rules as a moral good, not just a device to an end, and then enforce the system for its own sake, you had better hope that the rules are good ones, because you don't have a clue.

Key Command and Control Structures Examined in the Book.

First, the primary need of the leader is to maintain their position as leader. To do that, the village has to economically function. For the village to function, people have to (1) do things that they do not always want to do, and (2) do those things at times when they don't want to do them. So there has to be a command and control structure in place.

The people in the village have to participate as you, the leader, want. They may be forced to participate, or they may voluntarily participate. The best structure is when people voluntarily participate, because people are more effective when personally committed. Also, people will then police each other, putting the glue into the social bond. The freedom that people feel moving from the village to a large city is that release from the constant limits and rules that a small group imposes.

This chapter, brief as it is, points out some of the essential command and control issues that the next few chapters look at in more depth. The command and control structures attempt to structure behavior so it accomplishes what the leaders feel critical, which is quite different from what may be economically critical.

The following command and control structures are disassembled

and criticized in the following chapters, along with many other command and control structures.

- Village ethics are the basic rules to keep the group functioning.
  These rules are loaded with as much social/religious/ethical/
  moral force as possible, plus 10%, so that they cannot be examined or questioned. Powerful groups in society make their living
  from enforcing these rules.

- Morality plays are constantly thrown at the people to encourage/
  discourage behavior while keeping people entertained and passive.

- Virtues are encouraged behavior, so that you can police yourself,
  as well as the social community polices you.

- Vices are discouraged actions, again so you can police yourself,
  and give the neighbors names to call you.

- Selfishness is discouraged, because it diverts a persons focus from
  the group to themselves.

- Self destructive is carefully defined so that it is the social structure, not the individual, which is preserved.

- Monsters are defined so people won't consider certain possibilities.

Chapter 8: Village Ethics: Religious and Social Absolutes Defining the Box

What Are Village Ethics?

Village Ethics are simply the rules that the village has developed to keep the system going. The social contract trades individual skills for social resources. There are compromises in everything, which have to be accepted. What this book focuses on is the loading of those compromises with freight that isn't appropriate or necessary to the compromise, but which someone is profiting from.

For many reasons, over time, the essentially simple rules are overlaid with social, religious and ethical baggage out of proportion to basic rule. This is done for command and control purposes. It is absolutely critical to understand what the rules were for and discard much of the baggage they carry, so that they can be evaluated against the criteria of critical versus non-critical.

Village Ethics and Religion

"New opinions are always suspected, and usually opposed, without any other reason but because they are not already common."

—John Locke,
"An Essay Concerning
Human Understanding"

In what is likely a vain attempt to defuse religious issues, this book presents religion as both an individual spiritual exploration and a formal/informal social structure. The individual spiritual exploration is something each person must do for herself. The religious social structure is always co-opted into a command-and-control device, regardless of the society. This book looks at structures, regardless of where they come from, which are used as command-and-control methods for human behavior. Human-created structures are not divine, even if created through what the founders believe is the Will of the Divine.

This chapter looks directly at many of the basic social rules defining our worldview. It attempts to give perspective to the rules and where they came from, so that they can be thought about, dissected, and evaluated.

This chapter covers an enormous amount of ground in a short time. A full discussion of all the issues raised would require multiple volumes, so this is not a complete analysis by any means. The key point of this chapter is to illustrate how the village ethics are codified and layered with religious and other absolutes to coerce agreement.

The Ten Commandments

If you feel that examination of the divine word is wrong, you have to remember that the Word was originally written probably in early Hebrew, but possibly in other languages that no longer exist, and then translated back and forth between Aramaic, Greek, Latin, Hebrew again, and then English. All those languages have evolved over the centuries. What we now see as the word, those who originally wrote the word would certainly have intended at least somewhat differently.

This is emotionally dangerous ground for many people. Step back. You can believe these rules are divinely provided but still see that the rules have direct, often unexpected, results in the day-to-day functioning of a village. These rules are, in daily use, a structure for controlling people in a group. As such, in the real world, they are going to be applied and misapplied differently than the divinity likely would have intended.

If you can't examine the rules in their daily operation, then those who distort the rules for their own benefit have won without your even knowing. And if you can't conceive that your spiritual leaders on Earth would use the rules for their own benefit, then we're not sure how you got this far into the book.

Whether from early church teachings or other life experiences, people often see their God as a stern parent. To children, that is how they are presented, but as adults we need to move past those elementary concepts to a deeper spiritual understanding. So we are looking at how the rules are applied each day in this world, how systems evolve and change the relatively clear language, and how they are abused and misused constantly.

Commandments five to ten are a very close match for the Confucian rules, used as behavior guides in ancient/medieval China, and they are consistent with the rules for all small groups. If you were the village chief and had a blank sheet of paper (assuming you knew how to write) these are the rules you would create to keep the village intact.

In the daily operation of the village, rules always apply more to those lower in status, because they are subject to more social and physical control. The rules hardly apply at all to the relations between villages because of a lack of control mechanisms.

The commandments are as follows:

1. You shall not worship any other god but YHWH.

2. You shall not make a graven image.

3. You shall not take the name of YHWH in vain.

4. You shall not break the Sabbath.

5. You shall not dishonor your parents.

6. You shall not murder.

7. You shall not commit adultery.

8. You shall not steal.

9. You shall not commit perjury.

10. You shall not covet.[6]

The first four rules are clearly focused on religious aspects. From a practical standpoint, having everyone in the village share the same religion has many social cohesion advantages.

Every religion at its core must view non-believers as either

---

[6] King James Version

fools or the forsaken. Therefore, religious tolerance varies between extremes of either (1) considering the non-believers useless fools who are not wanted or needed in the religion, but tolerated if they perform some useful economic function, or (2) considering the non-believers vermin to be exterminated. A consistency in belief would certainly eliminate the tolerance issues. Note that we are completely avoiding any discussion of the religious aspects as religious truth; we are looking at daily operations.

Having said that, humans being what they are, the most vicious fights are usually between people in (nominally) the same religion over what seems to outsiders as trivial disagreements in theology. That occurs because the dissenters quickly fall into the "vermin" category, and since they are all generally geographically closely located, the friction is constant.

> "Society can overlook murder, adultery, or swindling;
> it can never forgive the preaching of a new gospel."
>
> —Frederic Harrison

Again stepping aside from the question of revealed truth, there is no question that the Ten Commandments are a good plan for daily living. From a feedback point of view, there are positive upsides and minimal negative downsides to all those behaviors. Life would have less worries and hassles, *except where the rules are manipulated out of their context as control mechanisms.*

Where you take an action, ripples from actions sometimes accumulate, and the next action or the one after that may fail because of those ripples from prior choices. The advantage to many of the village ethics rules is that the ripples from actions tend to be minimally negative. If your actions have positive upsides and minimal downsides, then typically your future choices and actions will not be constrained by the past actions, and you are in position for "luck" to help you.

Conversely, if your entire life is a variation on the theme of "Wow, we almost got it that time," then soon enough you won't skate. Choosing actions with minimal upside and substantial downside fights the mathematical reduction to the mean, and you will lose. Therefore, village ethics make sense as a general guide simply because of the weighing of high positive upsides to minimal negative downsides works to limit negative consequences.

Using the rules to then extend to norms and values that actually have almost nothing to do with the commandments as devised twists the system in favor of the manipulator. Because the rules are divinely ordained, questioning how they are applied (especially by those higher in the social order) becomes heresy. While that manipulation of the divine rules should clearly be some kind of sin, those who define sin tend to be the same group that is doing the manipulation.

Modern western society, while ostensibly secular in many ways, is firmly rooted in the Christian rules. The rules we are to live by, such as the long discourse on 'cooperation' in Chapter 10, are firmly religious based, even if not as overtly tied to their original religious background.

The Spanish considered themselves devoted defenders of the faith for centuries. In that defense, they were known for astonishing cruelties in the name of defending Christianity. For example, in the New World, they clearly ignored commandments six to ten in an intentional and systematic way, but they still were the "good."

Meta Village ethics, which is the application of the rules outside the village, is difficult because of control mechanisms. Elaborate layers of social and physical controls ensure the commandments are more or less adhered to inside the village. Outside the village, those command-and-control mechanisms don't exist. Outside the village, there are physical and economic command-and-control forces that make their own rules. The following quotation shows the type of thinking that frames strategy considerations by the leaders in village-to-village relationships:

> ". . . In affairs so dangerous as war, false ideas proceeding from kindness of heart are precisely the worst. As the most extensive use of physical force by no means excludes the co-operation of intelligence, he who uses this force ruthlessly, shrinking from no amount of bloodshed, must gain an advantage if his

adversary does not do the same. Thereby he forces his adversary's hand, and thus each pushes the other to extremities to which the only limitation is the strength of resistance on the other side.

This is how the matter must be regarded, and it is a waste—and worse than a waste—of effort to ignore the element of brutality because of the repugnance it excites.[7]

All wars start with parades and high intentions, and end with shooting children in the mud. Do you doubt you need your monster to deal with that kind of cold-blooded analysis at the top?

Confucian ethics

"As a foundation for the life of perfect goodness, Confucius insisted mainly on the four virtues of sincerity, benevolence, filial piety, and propriety ... Another virtue of primary importance in the Confucian system is "propriety." It embraces the whole aspect of human conduct teaching men to do the right thing. In the rules, ceremony, customs and usages are listed by which Chinese etiquette is regulated. *They were distinguished even in Confucius's day by the three hundred greater, and the three thousand lesser rules of ceremony, all of which had to be carefully learned as a guide to right conduct.* The conventional usages as well as the rules of moral conduct brought with them the sense of obligation resting primarily on the authority of the sage-kings and on the will of Heaven. To neglect or deviate from them was equivalent to committing a sin."[8]

---

[7]   Carl von Clausewitz, *On War* (Caleb Carr, series Editor, The Modern Library, 2000), 265.

[8]   Kathy Shinn, "Confucianism: A Brief Summary of Confucius and His Teachings," California State University, Chico, http://www.csuchico.edu/~cheinz/syllabi/asst001/fall97/11kshinn.htm (emphasis added).

To those more knowledgeable of the Confucian ethics, we apologize for the very quick summary presented. The key concept focused on here is the degree of formal structure, the very elaborate village ethics created.

Communism and the other "isms"

These are also a structure of village ethics, whose goal is more ambitious than just keeping everyone functioning. Under the socialist/ communist systems, human nature would actually be improved.

Socialism, essentially "from each according to his ability and to each according to his need," seems to be a political movement grown out of Christian ethics. That a system of that type didn't even work well in the monasteries should have given someone pause, but there were other political reasons for its popularity. Like all ideals, the problem that the world didn't seem to work that way was brushed aside.

Marx believed that socialism was an intermediate stage of social progress. The final stage would be communism. Under that structure, class differences would disappear, and people would live in harmony. Government, in the sense that government existed in his time, would be vastly diminished or non-existent.

All the Communist countries developed governments that controlled everything. Stalin's Russia was a sister to the Chinese empire in operation, despite the vast ideological differences, so Marx's concept was a dramatic failure.

Marx's dialectic was a complete, internally logical method for analyzing and dealing with the world, regardless of the situation. The dialectic was a tool to be used to reach the ultimate goals. So the true believer always had an answer and a plan. Unfortunately, the dialectic seemed to have very little relationship to reality, with the usual results. It is surprising how many people still accept it (perhaps because there is a great comfort in have something that explains everything, even if the explanation really doesn't work at all). Ironically, the failure of the dialectic, for some, increases its value. The system has to be right, just not understood and implemented correctly.

The net result of Marx's work really didn't seem to work at all well, as shown by the actual events in the ugly history of the twentieth century. There is nothing more dangerous than your wishes read into a social movement. For a leader, follow Groucho, not Karl.

The same examination could be made for other religious and cultural absolutes. I think it is clear, without going on for thousands of pages, that the rules are designed for the effective functioning of society, that the rules are not focused on the individual, and that those absolutes are constantly misused and twisted for non-divine purposes.

Chapter 9: Morality Plays: Entertainment for Control

This chapter focuses on knowing when you are being manipulated, and what is being fed to you.

A high percentage of what passes for entertainment is simply a morality play. Good wins, evil is punished, and everyone goes home with a warm feeling. In the 1960s and 1970s, public nudity was banned, except for artistic nudity, which not surprisingly expanded in definition.

The key to any successful morality play is the suffering of "evil." If they accept their wrongs at the end, all the better. The more they suffer, the fewer clothes they have to wear. Making young, attractive women who are partially dressed suffer satisfies multiple social goals, which works well for Hollywood.

To an alien unfamiliar with human society, the practical difference between the ballet and a topless bar would simply be a little more clothing and a better dressed audience. We, of course, know that there is no comparison because of the deep artistic meaning in the ballet. At one time, of course, the theatre and opera were forbidden, considered licentious and immoral, and ballet dancers had reputations akin to today's strippers, before the passage of time lent them acceptability. And, if the ballet or opera had terrible things happening to evildoers, then they wouldn't need everyone clothed all the time.

The key to any morality play is an appropriate straw man. Fill that straw man up, give him characteristics that people can identify with or against, and away it runs. The beauty of the straw man is that the actions and words the straw man uses are then combined in your mind, without question. So if an obviously dangerous person is saying rational things, the rational statements are then thrown out without consideration of their validity. Conversely, if respectable and reverent people are making statements that are nonsense, the nonsense is venerated and accepted.

By realizing which of the characters is the straw man, you can see what is being said. Maybe it makes sense, maybe it doesn't, but at least you are a participant. If you are going to dance to the beat that society is drumming, you should at least realize there is a song being played.

Morality plays then have suffering by the 'bad', and suffering by the 'good'. The acceptance of suffering by the hero lets us all accept the suffering in our life. Suffering is part of life. While the Princess Bride may have overstated by arguing that life is pain, it happens. But that doesn't mean pain and suffering should be worshipped, even sought after. Can't imagine that? Seeking penance through suffering is a historically a religious and social virtue. Giving up a pleasure for Lent is an example.

Recessions and depressions are rationalized on the (thin) grounds that the suffering and restrictions make people think and grow. That's true about the thinking and growing, but that doesn't validate the suffering. Now, if you chose your actions out of opposition to society, frustration, or a sense of "proving something" to someone, then your suffering plays well for society. If the suffering doesn't drive you back to the accepted, then you make a good example for others. That is why externalization has to be done carefully, or else you will be acting out the down side of another's morality play.

Police shows work wonderfully as morality plays. The format is ideal—social good versus social evil—and the real beauty is that forbidden actions can be tied to certain thoughts or concepts, whether there is any real relationship between them-the straw man in a uniform and badge. It is done so quickly that there isn't any question of proving the relationship between words and deeds.

For example, in a TV show, if you have an actor dressed as a senior member of a police force, intoning in a serious manner some social goal and the justification behind that goal, the mind just accepts what is being said as a statement of authority. The pronouncement from authority is not rationally evaluated, just absorbed. That the policy/goal may make absolutely no sense, but be founded in the personal needs of a person in power, never gets examined.

When the social preference works to the practical advantage of interlinked groups, it is very dangerous. The military-industrial alliance has been warned against, mostly unsuccessfully, for many years. Another critical interlinked group, the PPP (police/prosecutors/prisons) works together for what serves their personal interests as well as the social goals that they use for cover. Because of their position and power in society, then the nonsense gets very deep very fast. Only budget constraints can stand against them.

The secondary problem with police drama as morality show is that the police take themselves seriously as the guardians of all that is good and right, even when they are clearly out of their territory. So police 'find' evidence, manipulate evidence, and help the judicial system come to the 'right' answer, which is OK because the police are 'good' guys. Interference by the Judiciary is deeply resented.

The basic trick, discussed in this paragraph, which you should memorize and take seriously, is the heart of the police shows. The interrogation process is carefully designed, both on TV and in real life, to take regular social interaction—conversation between individuals—and turn it into a ghastly parody of that interaction. By that hijacking, and by the careful use of social markers and values out of context (for the benefit of the interrogator), the suspect plays play a role that is completely destructive to them, by providing information that will incriminate them. Watch for this trick, as it is played in many forums: police, jobs, any place where people seek to exploit their power. Police shows are a wonderful format for a morality play, which they are at heart, but you confuse them with real life at your risk.

Of course, the interrogation process is useful in many situations. And knowing how it works is critical! People being what they are, they will tend to use a useful tool in ways other than the tool was designed for. If you have a hammer, you will use a hammer for all kinds of things, especially if it gets agreement and support faster than actually having to address real needs or enlist people's minds and hearts.

How many other social situations are hijacked like this, with less obvious pressure, so that a person does what they are moved into doing? The essence of the process is first tying people to norms/markers, hijacking their vision of self, of their children, of their community, or of something else that they buy into, and then redefining them in the interaction so that the person is pushed into choices clearly at odds with what they may have thought was in their interest. If you are driving off the lot with a Corvette but what you really need is a car to carry stuff—and your three kids—then that car isn't going to work for you.

You just have to realize what is going on. If you are not in control of your thoughts, then someone else is. At that point, you can just hope your interests coincide.

If you want to see the village ethics in modern society, look at the tabloids. You can always apply an ethic out of context to make a person look foolish or wrong (and if you have Photoshop, all the more fun). People love to see other people look bad; maybe it helps them rationalize their life, makes them feels better, helps them deal with life's inherent conflicts. If you can't think of anything else, then go back into history and apply rules completely out of context to the situation for entertainment.

More subtly, village ethics, by creating a shared social reality, are used daily to hide whatever aspect of the real world seems to be most annoying. The group, and most dangerously, the leaders, start thinking that if everyone agrees on X, then X must be true, in all times and places. This works to a point, until the village walks into something hard that wasn't supposed to be there (that violates the rules!).

The recent economic downturn was really caused by social fictions: a group of people jumped off a tall building (real estate always goes up, and credit reports don't matter) and as they passed each floor, shouted to the people on that floor that things were fine. Unfortunately the people they shouted to, the regulators, the investors, and the bond rating agencies, among many others, bought into the concept. When the group hit the pavement, they brought us all along with them.

We all act out our personal morality plays, even when we are alone. We have appropriate facial expressions, which we use by ourselves when we think about the past and the future. One of the authors happens to like BMW automobiles a great deal, but one of the downsides to having a BMW is a tendency to have that "BMW look" while driving: the determined master of the universe.

We can all tell what is authentic in a movie and what isn't. When a movie consists merely of random actions that keep us involved visually, we can feel this and don't take it seriously. For example, *The Godfather* and *The Godfather: Part II* felt authentic and were wonderful movies. Greek tragedy redone in the modern world, as the Corleone's struggled against what they had to become and do. *The Godfather 3* felt like a succession of unlinked straw men written around popular moral points, and so the characters were puppets to make points, not people.

The continued difference between movie reviews and what people enjoy seeing is another example of morality play rules. Movie reviews play by certain intellectual and ethical ground rules, which don't seem tied at all to what people enjoy in a movie. Thus the endless headlines about what thoughtless movie is packed this weekend while the acclaimed bleak intellectual exercise in meaninglessness is empty.

The rules of literary criticism endorse social certain virtues and group think, because the reviewers accrue intellectual points and stay in the system that way. Not only do your reviews have to be well written, but they have to convince your superiors at the newspaper and in the profession that you are leading the pack. Because the creators of the movies have to score intellectual points, as well as make money, we get movies that are clearly fighting someone else's emotional battles, which we, the public, are supposed to pay for and enjoy.

Chapter 10: Virtue and Vice Are Ineffective and Outmoded Devices

> "Don't think you're on the right road just because it's a well-beaten path."
>
> —Anonymous

Opening up virtues and vices to examination is critical to finding your inner monster-and yourself. Virtues and vices are the controls carefully planted in all of us to implement the good/bad rules. Even in a secular society, those traditional concepts control our daily viewpoints. Discovering that you can evaluate them and pick your own controls is liberating. Unfortunately, it requires suffering through many pages of reading about them and their effects.

Village ethics are expressed through the virtues and vices of a group. Virtues are rewarded, both formally and informally. Virtues may be personally rewarding, but often they are not, which is the main reason for formal and informal rewards. Vices are punished both formally and informally, but they are often very personally rewarding, another reason that the individual can't be trusted in society's view.

> "Whenever you find yourself on the side of the majority, it is time to pause and reflect."
>
> —Mark Twain

What Is Virtue? What Is Vice?

According to the *Catholic Encyclopedia*, virtue can be understood as follows:

> According to its etymology the word *virtue* (Latin *virtus*) signifies manliness or courage. "Appelata est enim a viro virtus: viri autem propria maxime est fortitudo" ("The term virtue is from the word that

signifies man; a man's chief quality is fortitude";
Cicero, "Tuscul.", I, xi, 18). Taken in its widest sense
virtue means the excellence of perfection of a thing,
just as vice, its contrary, denotes a defect or absence
of perfection due to a thing. In its strictest meaning, however, as used by moral philosophers and
theologians, it signifies a habit superadded to a fac-
ulty of the soul, disposing it to elicit with readiness
acts conformable to our rational nature. "Virtue,"
says Augustine, "is a good habit consonant with our
nature." From Saint Thomas's entire Question on the
essence of virtue may be gathered his brief but complete definition of virtue: "habitus operativus bonus,"
an operative habit essentially good, as distinguished
from vice, an operative habit essentially evil.[9]

The challenge of this definition, applied to the world we face
every day, is that the definition of the various virtue's are skewed
towards what the economic and political systems need and wants.
What the divine word actually meant, as translated from language
to language over time, in different social and political contexts, becomes whatever the person controlling the system decides it means,
based on what is needed to control society.

Here is another definition:

"Virtue, in this Confucian view, is based upon harmony with other people, produced through this type
of ethical practice by a growing identification of the
interests of self and other.[10]

That is a wonderful, cheerful view of people working together in
harmony. In reality, the harmony actually resulted in a frozen social
structure evidencing harmony by complete control emanating from

---

9   Catholic Encyclopaedia, "Virtue," http://www.newadvent.org/cathen/15472a.
     htm.
10 Wikipedia, "Confucius," http://en.wikipedia.org/wiki/Confucius.

the emperor. The way things actually work is just one of those interesting things about humans. The writings of Sun Tzu, *The Art of War*, flowed from this same culture and are a more accurate reflection of the struggle of life in those times. Confucian virtues, unfortunately, seem to have been applied to very formally control the populace after *The Art of War* was applied to resolve the conflicts inherent with a group.

Because of the importance of harmony and fitting in, the concept of *face* flows from this tradition. Face is one of those definitions contained in the word: it is your appearance in the eyes of others.

Face is one of the most socially dangerous concepts because of the way it interacts with first-level thinking. First level thinking is an analysis that stops with the action and the social justification for the action. First level thinking doesn't look to actual consequences, it looks to social consequences. Therefore first level thinking is easy to defend. Unfortunately, basing real world decisions on social values makes the ultimate success of the action a throw of the die, but at least you can justify failure. Face, which in European cultures would be closer to image and/or ego, is clearly a command-and-control device. If you are obsessed with your "face" in the eyes of others, then you will clearly do what you think society wants.

In reality, the concept is tied to others' views, so you quickly fall into "he thinks I think he thinks..." mode. The typical solution to that thought pattern is simply to find something you want and decide that is what they wanted, justified in appropriate terms. The real problem is that combined with first-level thinking (only consider the action, not the consequences) people make decisions that end up causing more conflict and disruption in the system than if they were simply selfish.

For example, if the village needs the harvesting knives sharpened, but the sharpener is somehow insulted by the tone/terms/timing of the demand (or the demander committed some social offence against the sharpener's family), then the knives are not fully sharpened, because to comply completely with the request results in a loss of face among the most critical group the person is concerned about. The absolute necessity for sharp knives for the harvest is a consequence that isn't as relevant as the opinion of family.

Virtue is not doing something you want to do or are designed to do because of actual or perceived damage to the social structure. Chastity is so stressed for women because the operant hardware can easily handle multiple sex acts without strain or damage. Men would like to be as concerned with multiple sex acts, but the equipment just isn't made for it. Females actively engaging in multiple sex acts, which then necessarily means multiple males, absolutely tears the daily fabric of the village into pieces, and so there are many overlapping rules to keep that from happening. The African traditions of genital mutilation, even sometimes sewing the vagina shut, make it pretty clear which behaviors are allowed.

Traditionally, parents raised their daughters to discourage them from doing things that by the time they made their own decisions, they were too old to have the options. An eighteen-year-old woman making her own decisions outside the prescribed social rules has a much greater effect on the village men than a forty-five-year-old woman making decisions (don't yell at the author's about the way the world works) so that worked-at a considerable cost to the women involved.

A definition of vice is as follows:

> Vice is a practice or habit considered immoral, depraved, and/or degrading in the associated society. In more minor usage, vice can refer to a fault, a defect, an infirmity or merely a bad habit. Synonyms for vice include fault, depravity, sin, iniquity, wickedness and corruption. The modern English term that best captures its original meaning is the word vicious, which means "full of vice." In this sense, the word vice comes from the Latin word *vitium*, meaning "failing or defect." Vice is the opposite of virtue.[11]

And that lays it out with all the strength society can muster to discourage people. The concept brings in failure, defect, all the negatives that can be applied. And they are needed, because the vices

---

[11] Wikipedia, "Vice," http://en.wikipedia.org/wiki/Vice.

usually have actual positive rewards while we do them. Frankly, vices are what most of us want to do—eating, sleeping, sex, and thinking well of ourselves. In daily usage, whether an action is a virtue or a vice depends on the perspective of the observer, and the goal to be reached by the observer's judgment. This makes for a very flexible and useful command-and-control method, as long as you are in control of the judging.

Social Virtue versus Personal Virtue

This book draws a line between what society wants for its purposes and what you should want for your purposes. They are the same for many things, but absolutely not the same for many more. Society glosses over the difference between the absolutely necessary and the non-necessary, enforcing all of them through the same mechanisms. To reject their definitions of virtue is a type of virtue ("independence"), but you should not expect a lot of support from the outside when you oppose them. Virtue negates the individual for the social structure.

And you can't rely on the system to play fair when it is after something it sees as important. For example, a few years ago, repressed memory was the hot button, and many people's lives were destroyed by "recovered" memories of abuse that those people had allegedly committed on others. After a few years, brave researchers stood up and proved that the repressed memories were actually created/implanted memories by the prosecutors and psychologists, none of whom seem to have been punished for their actions. Because the concept accomplished many politically correct goals, those who used the concept were not held accountable. Those who were imprisoned were sometimes freed.

Some virtues, which are tied to absolutely necessary social actions, have to be accepted by the individual regardless of the consequences. The seed has to be planted in the ground at the right time, and the crop has to be harvested. Likewise, the virtues of hard work, timeliness, and honesty (not stealing the harvest) are necessary so that there will be a village tomorrow.

Virtue, like patriotism, can be the last refuge of the scoundrel. History is full of people frantically waving the bloody flag to distract people from what that person did or is about to do. Always watch the person who advertises himself as virtuous. Those who really are know that they try and fail. Only those who are not virtuous fully utilize the advantages of being seen that way.

The list of honored leaders and esteemed spiritual leaders who crash and burn from doing things they make a living attacking would make a continuing multivolume set of books of its own. And then there is the slow-moving train wreck of the Catholic Church and problem priests, which for any other institution would have resulted in many more indictments.

Sadly, the social virtue of tolerance doesn't work with the non-tolerant, who happily take what they want. There was a legendary Jewish sect a very long time ago that would not do anything, including fight, on the holy day. It didn't take the surrounding tribes long to work the implications of this out, with detrimental results to the sect. That is an example of an ideal concept gone berserk.

It is all that other stuff, the flotsam of historical events, the personal peeves and beliefs of the ruling class, the daily minute control of action and behavior to keep the group from thinking, that can and has to be examined—and in many cases rejected.

Virtue and Vice Are Socially Defined

That seems so obvious as to be a truism. It is important, though, because all truisms, while they vanish into the background in the discussion, shape the discussion by their existence. You have to back these out into the light to see what we are trying to challenge.

The book isn't denying that people have to work together on a daily basis, and because of that need to work together, certain behaviors are better than other behaviors. But the virtue and vice definitions take the necessary components and add far too much freight to the definitions, for command and control reasons. The book is arguing that the absolute dominance of society over the individual is not correct for all levels of conduct. We are arguing that the individual can examine those definitions and limit compliance to what is necessary for daily life, not taking on board all the freight that society wants to hand over. The problem is—and this is the reason your inner monster is so important—that all these definitions and values have piled in so fast and furious that you can't see past them. This is the "coral reef" buildup in a prior chapter.

Remember, we started out with the concept of "good is them, bad is you." That really isn't a surprise, if you think about it, but people don't think about the underlying social values. People start with the social values and run with them, which is the mistake. It is critical to understand your choices, not just to flip between conflicting ideals of virtue as they seem most convenient. While we're not arguing that Flashman (the literary character who is a notorious fraud, coward, and cheat) is to be imitated, there is a need to examine these virtues and vices.[12] By the way, if you do read Flashman, extend the concepts beyond the books. The Flashman books, which promote a rejection of society's ethics, don't really examine the ethics and why parts are rejected. The books simply reject parts to make a good read. An author can define the actions and consequences; applying choices to life is more difficult.

A recent formulation of the virtues and vices, from an article reported by Fox News on new mortal sins, says:

> Although there is no definitive list of mortal sins, many believers accept the broad seven deadly sins or capital vices laid down in the 6th century by Pope Gregory the Great and popularized in the Middle Ages by Dante in "The Inferno": lust, gluttony, avarice, sloth, anger, envy and pride.
>
> Christians are exhorted instead to adhere to the seven holy virtues: chastity, abstinence, temperance, diligence, patience, kindness and humility[13].

You, as a member of society, are supposed to aspire to those attributes every day in every way. The autosuggestion approach of Coue ("Every day, in every way, I'm getting better and better") was a

---

[12] See George MacDonald, *Flashman at the Charge,* (Plume, 1986), one of the several books in the series.

[13] Richard Owen, "Vatican Adds Seven New Deadly Sins, Including Damaging Environment and Drug Dealing" Fox News Web site, http://www.foxnews.com/story/0,2933,336330,00.html

deliberate device to reach those virtues. The mere fact that it would be impossible to comply with those conflicting virtues, in every situation and in combination with each other, seemed irrelevant.

It is the nature of people to make things more complex. The simplicity of the few virtues listed above has become, in our world, the long list shown at www.virtuesproject.com. There is virtue after virtue for a person to aspire to. We've picked one for our analysis purposes, *cooperation*:

> Cooperation – Cooperation is working together and sharing the load. When we cooperate, we join with others to do things that cannot be done alone. We are willing to follow the rules which keep everyone safe and happy. Together we can accomplish great things.[14]

There are a number of problems with this definition:

It is good for society and bad for us. You are cooperative within a socially defined set of limits, and your cooperation "grade" is based on approval from society. You cooperate with what you should cooperate on, in a socially allowed manner at the relevant times. Cooperation has been drummed into you since age two, and disagreeing with the proposed goal of the group isn't cooperation. Cooperation is shutting up and doing as you are told. Most importantly, implicit is the fact that you are doing what someone else wants. If you have thought through the effects on you, then okay. But cooperation is essentially doing what someone else wants for their purposes, and just because it has been made into a virtue does not mean it the best thing for your interests. That's *why* it is made a virtue. Cooperative is going along with command-and-control structures.

In many cases, cooperation is damaging to society as well. The present mess of the United States primary education system is chiefly

---

[14]   The Virtues Project, "What Are the Virtues?" http://www.virtuesproject.com/virtueslist.html.

due to the lack of checks and balances on the teachers and unions. The school districts, outmanned and often put in place with union backing, co-operate with the nominal educational goals, with the result that there isn't any pushback against whatever oddball proposal is pushed next. That the proposals usually result in better benefits and more time off for the teachers just seems to be one of those things.

Likewise, the American auto industry ignored the checks and balances in the economic system, to its ultimate dismay. The buyers, as the ultimate check and balance, were less important that the demands of the unions and the management, who cooperated to divide up the pie between them while there was still a pie. Periodically, they lashed out against the foreign automakers, who made a product that the buyers found superior, and who at the time refused to cooperate correctly.

The definition of cooperation is so unclear with respect to actions and measurable results that it is almost useless. What if you cooperate on things that authority wants but that some people don't like, such as being a guard in a concentration camp? "I was following orders" was a defense offered at Nuremberg, the Nazi war crimes trials. The defense was rejected by the victors but honored before the Nazis lost the war. The firestorm that destroyed Dresden was a choice of the victors, and not judged.

In Wealth of Nations (approx. 1760) Adam Smith said, "People of the same trade seldom meet together, even for merriment and diversion, but the conversation ends in a conspiracy against the public, or in some contrivance to raise prices." This certainly suggests cooperation between them. This doesn't seem to be virtuous cooperation, however, even when it increases employment and wages for the relevant economic groups.

How do you measure how cooperative parties are when goals are unclear or conflicting? And who is making the evaluation and passing out the rewards/penalties? This is the critical question.

The definition was defined according to historical situations and choices, which are often not relevant to a present choice. "Follow[ing] the rules which keep everyone safe and happy" covers a lot of ground. What if the rules really don't work, but you are supposed cooperate?

What if society is pretending something to keep people safe and happy? What is cooperation then?

Cooperation to keep everyone safe and happy works pretty well at recess in kindergarten, but the real world is more complex than that. Look at imperial China, where the Confucian ethics of cooperation, as applied, resulted in a mass cooperation and conformity that eventually destroyed the society.

Definitions of virtues have buried within them religious and ethical terms that cannot be examined without violating very serious social rules. Failing to cooperate means being thrown out of the group, which can include the religious structure a person has chosen. Certainly, being "uncooperative" is a sin, especially if based on pride, and serious, formally dressed people will weigh in against that behavior.

Being uncooperative when it comes to giving to the church is clearly a sin. Being uncooperative by refusing to support all the dogmas of any given church is blasphemy. Questioning the virtue and underlying issues is often a sin on its face.

Obviously, being cooperative is different at age four than at age ten and at age thirty, and it depends on whether it is with your spouse, your boss, or your co-workers. Being cooperative with the FBI when they are asking questions is a lot different from lending a hand to a friend, but one might think they are the same according to the wording above. And the FBI will look you straight in the face and demand that virtuous cooperation, even if it is completely destructive to you and your interests.

An interesting thing about cooperation is how damaging it can be to the ethical system. President Bush, based on reams of documents, entered into a war in Iraq on a false basis. He and his advisors clearly misrepresented and lied to a grieving American public, angry over 9/11 and seeking vengeance. In the process, Bush lost focus on the Taliban, which has resulted in them gaining strength again, and a position inside Pakistan that is more dangerous to American interest than before President Bush started. Yet President Bush's fundamentalist Christen backers did not rise up when the falsehood and dishonesty was disclosed, as virtue would demand. Why? The human ability to rationalize and smooth over certainly comes to mind. They were cooperating. Further, it is always dangerous to tie profit to ethics, and a repudiation of President Bush would have made more difficult many real-world relationships and other goals which that the churches had. Power corrupts, and absolute power corrupts absolutely.

And we could ramble on for pages and pages, looking at each example until every reader was deep in sleep.

The sad thing is that the people working on the virtues mean well, by traditional lights. Underlying their efforts is the idea that without all this "stuff," we would revert to barbaric behavior within a short time. Most of our social behavior is hard wired into us. People, placed in a group without social structures, create their own. Prisoners on an island create a structure. Even the "Lord of the Flies", which had a group of civilized boys rapidly go to barbarism, depicted barbaric actions as happening within a structure. It isn't the virtues and the guides that make us social, we pop out that way.

The key problem with the virtues and vices, as defined, is that they fail to distinguish the great (the critical behaviors to work together daily) from the small (someone's personal preferences).

There is no question that the listed virtues represent behaviors that are often necessary to minimize the frictions in daily life. However, we have all been taught these virtues, at different times and different places, generally with minimal examination of them. So what you learn at age five is different from age ten, fifteen, and thirty-five. Every parent knows that you blatantly lie to your children when they are young in a continued attempt to keep them alive. Those multiple definitions, outright falsehoods, full-, half-, and part-truths accumulate in our minds.

Imagine carrying the long list of virtues at www.virtuesproject. com with you one day, with the conscious goal of meeting all of them all the time. What a confused and frustrating day that would be, and the load for the confusion and discomfort is laid on you— *your* abilities are inadequate, *your* skills insufficient, *your* attempts incomplete.

"It is the act of a madman to pursue impossibilities."

—Marcus Aurelius Antoninus,
Roman emperor, A.D. 161–180

So the standard model of humans as creatures filled with massive forces fighting against each other is consistent with trying to comply with all of those inconsistent and incoherent virtues. If you get up every morning using impossible guides, you are going to be conflicted. The problem with trying to think things through, to develop goals and plans based on ourselves, is that the terms used to develop those goals are so socially biased and ignore so much of human nature, and the "you," that you can't move your mind outside to reach yourself.

This book, by focusing on the value of the individual, requires you to think about what is important to you, for you. That won't result in mass murder and bank robbery (neither of which we recommend, by the way). Real robbery is done with a pencil, not a gun, and best of all with a congressional budget bill. Real mass murder requires being elected to a position of power.

As humans, we do have definite innate social behaviors that other animals don't have, and a considerable portion of our mental apparatus is designed to deal with social situations. Therefore, there are very real limits to how much socialization a person can reject. But saying that there are built-in socialization parameters in the brain doesn't mean that you should not look at what you have been handed and determine what makes sense.

The key problem with the overabundance of virtues is that trying to hold in the mind a collection of contradictory and poorly defined guides results in frustration and exhaustion. To compensate, people pick and choose their virtues, à la carte. Because there isn't a mechanism to evaluate the virtues, the ones we chose off the tray presented to us are not often the best, either for an individual's goals or society's functions. Inappropriate results, confusion, and frustration breeds contempt of the system. The important virtue is ignored with the nonsense, and out goes the baby with the bath water.

Quadrant 1 Good for You Good for Society	Quadrant 2 Good for You Bad for Society
Quadrant 3 Bad for You Good for Society	Quadrant 4 Bad for You Bad for Society

The book seeks a radical change in the individual's relationship to society, which is shown in the above diagram. Quadrant 1, which is a 'good-good' for all parties, is probably the most desirable, but unfortunately limited in real life. Quadrant 3, which is good society/ bad individual, is the most common, with a considerable amount of effort expended by society to persuade the individual that this is really Quadrant 1. Quadrant 2 is the critical change that this book seeks. Outside the absolutely critical social requirements, which are far more limited than commonly presented, each person owes it to him or herself to think through what is good for them, even if society says it is bad. Quadrant 2 is much larger than society wants you to realize. Putting yourself in Quadrant 2 means that you may not be as productive or conformist as society (or at least certain segments of society) wants.

Quadrant 4 is a lose-lose, and a bad place to be. People are in Quadrant 4 more than they might want, because they see themselves in opposition to society. By rebelling, in socially defined terms, their image to the social world is clear, but completely defined by society. You may have decided to be the bad side of the morality play, but you didn't think through what the play is about. Bad for you is bad for you, regardless of how other's may view it.

So we are asking you to rethink whether a particular 'virtue' is actually good for you, and whether a particular 'vice' is actually bad for you. As each virtue and vice will combine some good and some bad aspects for you, split those apart so you can make your decision on what is good or bad for you. You don't have to take the packages as a whole: you can ask what works for you and what doesn't.

The diagram recasts the fixed view of virtue and vice. For any given virtue, the usual analysis is that it is good for society, and to some degree good for the individual, if in no other way than the individual does not run afoul of society's sanctions. Vices would be the reverse.

This diagram rejects the key assumption that society is always more important than the individual. The diagram conceptually shows that that some virtues are bad for the individual, while they may be good for society, and some vices are good for the individual, while they may be bad for society. You have to think whether it is good or dangerous for the person or society.

Simply going with the standard "good/dangerous for society" paradigm lets society run free, imposing any requirements it desires on the individual. Of course, the next question in making choices is the relative importance of the social demand to social functioning, and of course, for externalizations, what the control mechanisms are. Social demands related to critical functions with armed forces behind them have to be considered very carefully. Social demands related to whims enforced by other individual's discretionary approval are not generally as serious, but still take thought.

This chapter largely falls into the 'demolition' category of construction. The rejection of pat virtue/vice definitions urged in this chapter allows you to open up and feel yourself. It is absolutely essential for finding your inner monster, as otherwise you are trapped in the definitions. 'Vice' is examined in much greater depth in the next chapter.

CHAPTER 11: MONSTROUS BEHAVIOR: VICE

As society defines the good as them, and monsters are the bad (you), we need to look through the typical depictions of monsters to see what is really being hidden by being pushed onto the monsters. Monster's by definition do prohibited things. Vice's are social shorthand for prohibited behaviors, and so this chapter focuses on vice.

Vices are reviled because they are powerful and real to people. Vices are actions/thoughts/feelings resulting from what we are as humans, as opposed to economic production entities. What is described as virtue/vice arises from our nature, but is sorted out based on social functioning. Good is them is virtue, and bad is you is vice.

Think about what you could accomplish if you could draw on the raw power and passion of the forbidden vices. Vices are carefully defined to combine something authentically damaging to yourself and actions/thoughts/beliefs that seem to harm society, or at least some parts of society. As things accrue over time, any particular vice definition will carry as much social freight as the word will bear, plus 10 percent.

As you read the following forbidden actions, can you imagine embracing these sins as strengths? Can you imagine bringing yourself together, not pushed apart into segments?

The following is focused on western culture, but all cultures ban (at least for the masses) essentially the same behaviors. A constant refrain is that in considering these definitions, you have to weed out those that are tied to critical group functions, and those that are the non-critical stuff for command and control. Cynically, behaviors that waste resources (as they are being enjoyed) and keep people from getting that harvest in are always going to be a vice.

Thinking about Virtue and Vice

In considering the vices, you have already sinned, by thinking and challenging the definitions. That thought process is forbidden, because it fences off the options. There are some theological exceptions, such as for finding the truth, but those are limited to the elect. The elected know where their bread is buttered before they start.

Secondly, there are many behaviors mixed into the vices that are physically harmful to yourself, just as there are many behaviors mixed into the vices that are harmful only to certain perceived social functions, although they may be quite healthy and helpful for you.

Combining the "harmful to you" and "harmful to them" works well for command-and-control purposes. If you do as you are told, the allowed behaviors are usually physically good for you. Take bravery, for example. As long as you're not running into machinegun fire, it will usually serve you well in life. If you don't do as you are told and embrace the prohibited behaviors, at least some of them will be harmful to you. Drinking too much, sex with the wrong people, and thoughtless violence (bar fights) all have some upside, but some very high downside as well. Either you will come back to what is allowed, accepting all the rules as useful without examination, or you will be a horrible example for the others of what not to do.

What the system doesn't anticipate is that you will think about these vices, weeding out the 'harmful to you' from the 'harmful to peripheral interests of society' and making intelligent choices yourself. Unfortunately, weeding out all the nonsense can seem like an overwhelming task. It is the core of this book that your monster does that weeding daily; you need to find and understand the monster to find yourself.

The fallback impassioned defense of the virtues, even where successfully argued that something doesn't work/make sense, is that it's the system. You either buy the system completely or you do not, because if everyone started making decisions, then there would be chaos. That is true when it comes to the critical elements of cooperation, but not true in all cases.

The final grandstanding defense of the system, that it is so weak that even the slightest examination or question of it will plunge us all into the pit, just doesn't make sense except that the system knows a lot of the rules are optional. Once people realize some rules are optional, unless they have a structure to analyze things, they may assume they are *all* optional, and then you do have chaos. By failing to teach a method to analyze the system and determine what's critical, allowing people to make choices where they can, the system forces all-or-nothing.

Vices

Monsters are then:

Lustful,
Gluttons,
Greedy,
Lazy/Slothful,
Wrathful,
Envious,
and Proud

These are the Seven Deadly Sins. The Seven Deadly Sins are not to be confused with the Seven Dwarfs, who are Dopey, Grumpy, Doc, Happy, Bashful, Sneezy, and Sleepy. There is a book "The Seven Habits of Highly Effective People, a legend of the Seven Wonders of the Ancient World, and actually lots of 'seven' somethings, because we are hard wired to keep at most seven things in mind. If we were wired differently, there would probably be a list of fourteen or forty-three sins to work our way through.

This is serious, though, because those vices are the whips used to keep us in line.

The following looks at common definitions of the seven deadly sins, which most of the other vices are based on. There are hundreds of books written on each of these topics and subtopics, and so it is easy to be distracted down alleys. We are trying to focus on the essential concepts, condensed into a few pages.

Anger/Wrath

Wrath (or anger) may be described as inordinate and uncontrolled feelings of hatred and anger. These feelings can manifest as vehement denial of the truth, both to others and in the form of self-denial, impatience with the procedure of law, and the desire to seek revenge outside of the workings of the justice system ... and generally wishing to do evil or harm to others. The transgressions borne of vengeance are among the most serious, including murder, assault, and in extreme cases, genocide. Wrath is the only sin not necessarily associated with selfishness or self-interest (although one can of course be wrathful for selfish reasons, such as jealousy, closely related to the sin of envy). Dante described vengeance as "love of justice perverted to revenge and spite." In its original form, the sin of wrath also encompassed anger pointed internally rather than externally…[15]

Wrath is what monsters are good at; every monster you ever saw in a movie was angry at someone at some point. As in any good morality play, the monster's wrath was its destruction, but not before a good time was had by all watching the chaos.

Anger is critically important to you. You are taught to reject anger, because anger disturbs the group. Anger means that you are focused on you, not the needs of the group. You are taught this from elementary school.

Anger can't be rejected because it is essential to growth. Listen to your anger. It isn't pleasant, and it means something has to be done, but it won't go away. Anger is a shout, a plea, a cry for attention, for respect. But society doesn't want you to listen to anger, because you are likely to think to try and change what is making you angry.

Anger shows when you hit a boundary. Anger is the result of touching an electric fence holding you back. Anger shows you what you want. Anger shows where you want to go. Anger is what our ancestors used to keep them alive, and it is powerful. Anger tells you when you went somewhere and you didn't like it. You didn't like the way you were treated, what you were told.

Anger points the way to what you want. It is literally screaming inside you, telling you what you want. Anger that you feel is healthy. Anger that you can no longer feel is depression, denial, anger going within, against yourself.

Anger is to be acted upon, *not* acted out. That is all the difference. You can, and should be, raging and seething about what is important

---

[15]   http://en.wikipedia.org/wiki/Seven_deadly_sins

to you, but that doesn't mean it incoherently flows out of you, like a lightning bolt. If you are Zeus, then you can fling lightning bolts. If you are not, the bolts will burn your fingers. Anger points the direction for where you want to go. Anger is rocket fuel to drive you where the anger points you. It isn't to be wasted in explosions and useless acting out. Anger isn't the action; anger is the invitation to action. Anger is the impetus to find what's wrong and start fixing it.

Many studies provide sound bites that anger is bad for your blood pressure, that being happy is better. The small print in these studies says that bottled-up anger passing as happiness is the worst of all for you, but since society prioritizes its own ideals, you are to remember that anger is bad, and no subtleties allowed. How many grouchy old people do you know: if being angry killed people, they would be gone long ago. Anger will tell you when you have been betrayed. Anger is the most painful when we have betrayed ourselves. Betraying yourself can happen so quickly and often that you don't even have to notice, except for that anger inside that you numb.

Anger is the firestorm that cleans out the past life and opens the soil for the new. For years, Smoky the Bear said "No forest fires," and as a result, the woods became so overgrown that the inevitable fire completely destroyed the woods. Frequent small fires clear out the scrub and leave the trees to grow strong. Burning off the prairies on a regular basis put nutrients back in the soil and created space for the new grass. Banning or denying your anger has the same effect: if you hold it too long, it will consume you when it hits. Feel that anger a lot, make those necessary changes, and don't be consumed by the accumulation of all that stuff building up. Anger is a friend; anger is yourself shouting for your interests.

Ignore, reject, and deny anger, and it will go away. It will become sloth, despair, resignation, and depression. Those are the living dead of the soul, movement without feeling, dead eyes staring out. That *is* scary.

Pride

Pride is excessive belief in one's own abilities, which interferes with the individual's recognition of the grace of God. In almost every list pride (or hubris

or vanity) is considered the original and most serious of the seven deadly sins, and indeed the ultimate
source from which the others arise. It is identified
as a desire to be more important or attractive than
others, failing to give compliments to others though
they may be deserving of them ... and excessive love
of self ... In perhaps the best-known example, the
story of Lucifer, pride was what caused his fall from
Heaven, and his resultant transformation into Satan.
[16]

Pride goeth before a fall, and it is certainly true. The problem
with pride, in daily operation, is that it means you doesn't look outside; it defines what you want regardless of what actually is (always
a bad move) for monsters or for people. Pride is a social sin, which
means that you are functioning as the tool of those around you—you
need them to define you. Your pride depends on your relationship
to them, so they own you. Thus you are enmeshed in social reality, to
the exclusion of what is happening out there.

Pride, to the system, is the primary sin, because it allows you to
think for yourself. That just isn't allowed. Lucifer thought for himself, and look how that turned out. You have to be careful about
pride: pride that you are doing the opposite of what they want is still
in the system. Acting within and against the system means that you
are on track to be an example.

Pride is also a funny thing—it seems to depend on your point of
view of the sin being committed. One of the authors was at a summer
art fair this year, and he walked by a small group of normally dressed
people, who were praying to God to bring down fire and destruction on the place and the people at the fair. They were not kidding.
Perhaps he should have asked why, but they seemed rather focused.
We're sure they didn't see any sin of pride, but doesn't it seem as
though their determination of who needed to be punished is some
kind of elevation of their abilities and place in the cosmos? Weren't
they in fact committing the sins of wrath, envy, lust (for violence),

---
[16] http://en.wikipedia.org/wiki/Seven_deadly_sins>

and slothful discontent shown there? It was very Old Testament; you have to give them that.

Envy

> Envy is the desire for others' traits, status, abilities, or situation. "Love is patient, love is kind..." Love actively seeks the good of others for their sake. Envy resents the good others receive or even might receive. Envy is almost indistinguishable from pride at times.[17]

Envy is being discontented. Socially, envy is a sin if you want to be the lord of the manor, not the peasant in the hovel. Envy is a sin if you want something more than a person in your class should have (as determined by others). Envy is also personally destructive if you focus your life on something someone else has, thus making him or her the decision maker in your life.

Envy isn't just a human trait, by the way. Friederike Range, of the University of Vienna, found that dogs will shake hands for free as long as the human wants to, *until* the dogs observe other dogs getting treats for shaking, at which point the non-treated dogs will stop offering their paws and become agitated. Chimpanzees and certain monkeys will also stop cooperating if others receive treats for what they are doing for free. How that plays into free will and the uniqueness of the human spirit would be an interesting theological discussion.

Envy may be shouting at you that you gave up something you wanted and could have had. Others have it. They are happy. Why did you give it up? Was it for lack of money, advanced age, family and friends' opinions, other constraints? You denied yourself a luxury you wanted, and now others have it and they seem happy, so why did you do it? Envy shouts at you, and society wants you to push it away, because you probably gave the important things up for society. How were you repaid?

---

[17] http://en.wikipedia.org/wiki/Seven_deadly_sins>

If you can't give yourself time, then you eventually abandon yourself. To the outside, you look like you are there, but the true self has gone to ground. All that is left is the routine. And then envy is shouting inside about what you abandoned, and you are not supposed to listen to it.

Do you avoid thinking about what you want because you suddenly feel envious, and think envy is a forbidden sin? The problem with the book *The Seven Habits of Highly Effective People*, which wants people to start with their high-level goals and work down to daily actions, is that society's goals are blocking your actual self goals. If the real self doesn't buy the official self's goals, then the actions never follow, because the goals are not yours. They are just markings on a piece of paper without emotional engagement.

Gluttony

Gluttony is an inordinate desire to consume more than that which one requires. Temperance accepts the natural limits of pleasures and preserves this natural balance. This does not pertain only to food, but to entertainment and other legitimate goods, and even the company of others.[18]

Gluttony is one of the sins that is easy for the elected to preach on. Gluttony has some very obvious physical downsides. The problem is that the natural limit of pleasure is hard to determine. What if your stomach is full of the type of bacteria that cause obesity? Are you a glutton, or are the bacteria?

Gluttony is a good command-and-control mechanism, because overindulgence is an effective numbing device to cover up other problems. So the person is frustrated and can't articulate it, and to relieve their frustration eat too much. Now they can be blamed for being a glutton and no one ever has to deal with their underlying anger and frustration. A little hard on the person, but the system wins again.

Being a glutton generally means consuming more than one

18 http://en.wikipedia.org/wiki/Seven_deadly_sins

requires. So there is a measurement process at work, which measures calories in, calories out, perhaps types of calories, and an underlying reference as to ideal size. So you are measuring some set of actions and choices. The problem with measuring is that the devil is in what is being measured.

For example, accounting techniques are a system of checks and balances, but they only balance what is measured. What are you measuring and tracking? Humans have to measure and rate things: look at the way baseball statistics are collected, for example. Everything that can be measured objectively and reduced to a number is happily complied. But just because something is measured and rated doesn't mean that the information is useful. Baseball has discovered new statistical analyses in the last few years that rejected the prior measures that were thought to be the most important. The same seems to be occurring in basketball.

One of the clearest examples of a measurement assessment, obsessively pursued and almost completely useless, is the evaluation of breast size by males in selecting mates. The relationship of breast size to caring, intelligence, internal strength, and a host of really important criteria is close to nil, but there they are, easily capable of objective measurement.

So think about your evaluation criteria: just because you are measuring something doesn't mean the measurement is useful. And if you have a measurement that is useful for limited purposes, such as breast size, be careful about extrapolating that measurement to other matters that are important but really not related to the measurement you have. If you are not measuring what matters to you, then you are just making marks. Pointless marks create frustration. To push off the frustration, then you will do numbing things, and gluttony is one of the best.

Lust

Lust is an inordinate craving for the pleasures of the body. Self control and self mastery prevent pleasure from killing the soul by suffocation. Legitimate pleasures are controlled in the same way an athlete's muscles are: for maximum efficiency without damage.

Lust is the self-destructive drive for pleasure out of proportion to its worth. Sex, power, or image can be used well, but they tend to go out of control.[19]

The real problem with lust is that an inordinate craving is one thing while one is aroused and something vastly different afterwards. Lust is a favorite sin of the young, when the fires burn strong. It also is probably the most feared, next to anger, by the village. Lust tears the social fabric so quickly and thoroughly because people get their feelings hurt, which remain after the lust fades. Then comes anger. Lust has some of the same numbing effects as gluttony, which it is conceptually related to.

Lust is a problem for the social order, but also an opportunity. People, especially females, having indiscriminate sex is really going to mess up the structure and get the group upset. Are men getting upset at women making their own choices? Have men started killing each other? Then just give women no choices, and solve that problem. The damage to the individual is collateral.

The people making the rules tend to be older, so the fires have burned down a bit, and they can restrict their actions without any real effect to themselves, and they get that warm feeling of responsibility and control. Most importantly, if you are going to set rules that sow confusion among people, so that they have to rely on your choices for their emotional comfort, you want them twisted about sex, because when the urge comes back, and they are bound to you more each time.

Sloth

More than other sins, the definition of sloth has changed considerably since its original inclusion among the seven deadly sins. In fact it was first called the sin of sadness or despair. It had been in the early years of Christianity characterized by what modern writers would now describe as melancholy: apathy, depression, and joylessness—the last being viewed as

[19] http://en.wikipedia.org/wiki/Seven_deadly_sins>

being a refusal to enjoy the goodness of God and the world he created. Originally, its place was fulfilled by two other aspects, acedia and sadness. The former described a spiritual apathy that affected the faithful by discouraging them from their religious work. Sadness (tristitia in Latin) described a feeling of dissatisfaction or discontent, which caused unhappiness with one's current situation [emphasis added). When Thomas Aquinas selected acedia for his list, he described it as an "uneasiness of the mind," being a progenitor for lesser sins such as restlessness and instability...[20]

The sin of sloth, as originally conceived, would be a direct attack against a book like this—and all of modern society. The mere fact that people live longer, in better conditions, probably is irrelevant to the issue. Acting for yourself, thinking for yourself, being discontented, is exactly what the sin is trying to avoid. It is a deadly sin to be discontented with your present situation. (Bad Peasant) The sin makes restlessness and instability not socially acceptable because it obviously discomforts the elect. If people can think for him or herself, then the peasants/helots/serfs may not want to harvest, or move somewhere else. What would the lords do then?

Sloth, or despair, is a sin against yourself. By not acting, you lose time, which is all any of us really have.

Greed

Greed, like lust and gluttony, is a sin of excess. However, greed (as seen by the church) is applied to the acquisition of wealth in particular. St. Thomas Aquinas wrote that greed was "a sin against God, just as all mortal sins, in as much as man condemns things eternal for the sake of temporal things." "Avarice" is more of a blanket term that can describe many other examples of greedy behavior. These include disloyalty,

---

[20] http://en.wikipedia.org/wiki/Seven_deadly_sins

deliberate betrayal, or treason … especially for personal gain, for example through bribery. Scavenging and hoarding of materials or objects, theft and robbery, especially by means of violence, trickery, or manipulation of authority are all actions that may be inspired by greed. Such misdeeds can include simony, where one profits from soliciting goods within the actual confines of a church.[21]

It's greed when they profit from you and good business when you profit from them. Greed, and the acquisition of wealth through the economic structure, is what makes the system work. But setting up greed and mixing in other behaviors into the general definition makes it a very effective command-and-control device.

People naturally accumulate things. By giving some things to the "right" groups, you remove the element of sin, which works well for people with things. Some of the prohibited actions are critical to society and the individual: bribery, for example, is destructive of the village system and something that can't be allowed. Theft, robbery, and manipulation of authority for personal gain are all violations of the critical values of society and the individual.

Virtues and Vices as Command and Control

As you read these, did these definitions differ from what you understood the sins to be? When was the last time you thought about how these are spun into getting you to buy something, or not do something you thought made sense?

Pulling back from the close examination of the definitions, how often are these completely ignored and irrelevant to daily life? There seems to be an unwritten recognition of the distinction between what is critical and what isn't, and what isn't critical is then done. So people don't pay the payroll taxes on household employees, because it really doesn't matter. Woe betides those who get caught in the act, however-pay the household employee payroll taxes if you want to run for public office. But without thinking through what is critical

---

[21] http://en.wikipedia.org/wiki/Seven_deadly_sins>

and what isn't, people just fall into the roles provided, which are not set up for their good.

In the early Christian Church, there was a complete rejection of the material world for the life to be. The rejection of the material world, in the context of the collapse of civil society—the deprivations of the successive waves of barbarians, culminating with the Huns—made a certain amount of sense. Rejecting the material world, which was a pretty painful place, was a voluntary choice people made for their spiritual growth.

You were to live by rejecting the material world to prove your worth for the life to come. As there is a lack of direct contact with the almighty, the rules are necessarily provided by other humans. Rules, regardless of their source, in this world are expanded and modified by people. Monks and celibate churchmen are not going to create rules that show their lives as pointless. People being what they are, when they make rules, they ensure it is *your* life that is pointless.

The theological principles underlying that rejection of the material world also function very well as command-and-control mechanisms, and so they were co-opted for that use by the church and social structure. The sins presented above are a complete rejection of everyday life, and deliberately so.

There was a historical context to the rules at the time they were created, which has almost no relationship to the present world. Key parts of church dogma were clearly political compromises tied to friction between Constantinople and Rome, after the fall of the Western Roman Empire. Google "Ecumenical Councils of the Church" for a lot more material, which has been written about in hundreds of books.

Modern society involves different political realities and doesn't subscribe to the medieval worldview behind the early definitions of those sins. But your daily behavior still uses these rules as important values and markers, and they still work to sow confusion and indecision.

The rules were supposed to be impossible to follow—that was their design and function. They were for spiritual purity, transformed into command-and-control methods. In this world, things and systems change. On a daily basis, impossible rules result in confusion and paralysis, resulting in people looking for guidance and direction. That works well for the system. The daily application is disconnected from the theological underpinnings, but the end justifies the means.

The "logical" part of your mind, which carries all these rules in as coherent a system as it can, often is just a censor out of frustration. It is a constant stream of subversive remarks against what you are going to do. If doing something brings conflict, then don't do it, and here are fourteen reasons why no one does it, and the two people who did it were punished. As all actions conflict with some of the virtues, then life rapidly becomes a matter of choosing the lesser of two evils and carrying the burden for having chosen.

"The Inner Game of Tennis" [22]focuses on self 1 and self 2. Self 1 is the controlling part, that fusses and evaluates. Self 2 is the non-verbal, functioning part, the true self. The essence of the book is to get Self 1 to butt out and let Self 2 live. From this book's perspective, Self 1 is carefully trained to control, keeping Self 2 (your inner monster) down.

The mechanics of keeping track of sin violations—including sins of thought, action, omission, commission, individual and conspiracy, combinations and weights assigned to parts of the combined sins—imply a data collection and data mining process that boggles the mind. Father Guido Sarducci (comedian Don Novello) had a routine that proposed an accounting mechanism, which would be far more complex than the page St. Peter supposedly used to review his decision. The mere fact that no one could follow those rules meant that you had to hope that administrative discretion was going to be on your side. Thus, those who made their livings in the material world controlling you by the rules would have quite a wide area to work with.

Why should virtue be the negation of "you"? Why should sin be doing what you were made by the creator to do, act, and feel? You are a unique creation, with abilities and opportunities. Why would your creator want you to use none of that? It is clear why the social system

---

[22]   W. Timothy Gallwey, The Inner Game of Tennis, New York, Random House
      Paperbacks, 2008

would want obedience, and why they would write the rules in that way, but step back from the indoctrination and think.

The poor reader may be asking, "Why all this discussion that doesn't have lots of pictures of monster's, preferably with half-dressed people next to them? And why tilt against ancient definitions of sins?" Because those ancient definitions, frozen from an economic and social structure long since vanished, are still the basis for behavior guides today. If you don't look at where it comes from, you can't see where it is going and why it is wrong.

Those ancient rules are the foundation of what monsters are, and why you are being set up by the system so you act as it needs you to.

> Some things we are scared of and we should be scared of.

> Some things we are scared of, but we shouldn't be scared of.

> Some things we should be scared of that we are not scared of.

However, it is not the *things that they tell us about* that we should be scared of; it is *what they tell us* that we should be scared of. We are told that the rules are created in *good faith* for our protection.

> Good faith is an abstract and comprehensive term that encompasses a sincere belief or motive without any malice or the desire to defraud others. It derives from the translation of the Latin term bona fide, and courts use the two terms interchangeably.[23]

Their "good faith" was actually based on a complete rejection of life on Earth. That is the complete opposite of what we would

---

[23]   http://Answers.com, Law Encyclopedia, www.answers.com/topic/good-faith

consider good faith if your focus is living here and now. So saying that the rules were created in good faith to guide us in our daily lives in the material world today is simply incorrect. The rules were created, and contemplate, the complete rejection of the material world. The rules function well for the political and social systems to use as control-and-command devices, because they are impossible to implement.

Good Faith with Yourself

Having condemned society for not keeping good faith, you have to maintain good faith with yourself. If your reason for reading this book was to rationalize a good drunk, a fistfight with someone smaller, or intimate relations with your neighbor's spouse on Saturday night, then you are not thinking this through. You may be in touch with certain feelings, but not good faith with yourself.

Any fight, for example, has so many downsides for the emotional upside of victory—an emotional upside that is largely, if not entirely, an externalization of socialization behaviors—that it is extremely unwise. We have known many bricklayers over time, who generally tend to be thin, healthy people, typically pleasant and agreeable. They also lift heavy weights all day long, and they can pretty much tear the arms off regular people. One of the most polite young men we have ever met had just finished Special Forces training for the army, and he was as dangerous as a human could possibly be. So fighting with strangers is risky, and fighting with people you know is even worse. When you fight with people you know, if you lose, they will make fun of you tomorrow, and if you win, they can send the police to your house.

A "good drunk" is a phrase that makes sense semantically, but it doesn't describe anything that exists in reality. The advantage of language is that this pattern is pretty common, and society uses it all the time, but don't fool yourself. And that little adventure with your neighbor's spouse, other than acting out almost the full panoply of social virtues and vices in a short time, a classical hand written, as it were, morality play, doesn't make sense outside for your real interests.

CHAPTER 12: MONSTROUS BEHAVIOR: SELFISHNESS/SELF-DESTRUCTION

This chapter sets the stage for two important ideas essential for feeding your inner monster. First, that one has to be selfish, but there is good selfish and dangerous selfish, which each of us has to evaluate. Secondly, Self Destruction is vastly different than what is pitched at us by the command and control structure.

Monsters Are Selfish

Monsters are selfish. They don't sacrifice themselves for the good, or, more accurately, another's good. Society wants you to be a puppet on a string, and puppets are disposable. It is selfish for you to think you are not disposable. Selfishness is not sacrificing yourself by working yourself to death in the fields. Selfish is thinking about what you want, instead of what you are told is right to do.

We are all asked for sacrifices all the time; it is part of the social compact. You should think about and assess the sacrifice being requested, and ask why the other person doesn't just do it himself. we can promise you that the person asking for your sacrifice does *not* feel it as deeply as you will, despite his earnest statements to you. And in the rare event he does feel it as deeply, run away, because he is crazy. Why would a person take that level of punishment?

Selfishness is what makes democracy, as a system, work. Selfishness means that each person looks out for his own interest and votes in that way. While the campaigns make all kinds of social appeals, in the end, a person has a choice that they make based on their views.

Selfishness is what makes personal property such a powerful social device. People will work and slave over their personal property. If people don't have an ownership interest, whether legal or just emotional, nothing gets done. The housing projects in the major cities became havens for crime because no one felt an ownership interest to protect the common areas. If you own a house, no one walks in your yard, and you will take aggressive action to stop them. So your yard is safe, well kept, and flowery. The common areas in housing projects are decorated with graffiti, unconscious bodies, and waste products because no one had ownership (except the bureaucrats, and they went home at five).

When you rent a car, do you carefully listen to the odd little noises it produces? Do you put in the best gas? Do you carefully wipe up the Coke spills? No, because it isn't yours. Selfishness is what makes you take care of your things and do the right thing with those things.

We should be glad that we are selfish and have the good sense not to give ourselves completely to whatever someone else thinks of. If we didn't, you can rest assured that whoever is pulling the levers would find more for us to devote ourselves to than there is time in the day—or health in your body—to do.

Alexander Solzhenitsyn, in the Gulag Archipelago, talked about young, strong people sent to the Gulag who worked as hard as they could to prove they were there by mistake. They worked themselves to death, while those who carefully preserved their strength and held back where they could had a chance of survival.

If you are not selfish with your life, you invest more in the lives, hopes, and plans of others than in your own life. You detour your own life, for your perception of what others want. Since you don't know what you want, it seems unlikely you really know what they want, and a cycle of frustration continues. If you are not selfish enough to find time to rest and rebuild yourself, then when people you care about come to you for help, you are too tired to help.

Selfishness gets a bad rap in the common press, which really isn't justified. According to the *Oxford Modern English Dictionary*, to be "selfish" means to be "concerned chiefly with one's own interest."

Notice that the definition contains no ethical evaluation, either positive or negative. Selfish, as defined above, is the life model for a saint or a fiend. How? A saint lives the life he believes is in his best interest—as does the fiend, we assume. So selfishness isn't the operant issue; it is the perception of the individual as to their best interest. That is a combination of a person's internal wiring and the situation he sees himself in. Robin Hood was a fiend to the nobles and a saint to the peasants.

It is normally against your own interest to harm others-unless they are about to harm you. Unless you are Stalin, you harm others at your own risk (and it even caught him eventually). Behaving brutally or irrationally is a self-defeating practice. When your acts have significant downsides and limited upsides, life is going to go south fairly quickly.

Your inner monster wants you to live for your own sake rather than for the sake of others. You, as an individual, are the "bad," and your monster is that shoved-away "bad" that the social structure has defined. The monster is "selfish" by society's standards.

Obviously society wants you to live for others—it's good for them, being the others, and it puts you under society's complete control. If you challenge society, within its rules, and follow the defined deviance patterns, then your "selfish" actions will have the negative consequences society said they would, because they set this one up. Society has lots of devices for people to numb themselves and zone out. You have to think for yourself; you have to define your interest and your goals so that you are not just reacting to a set of rules designed to make you fail.

> "Be wary of the man who urges an action in which
> he himself incurs no risk.".
>
> —Lucius Annaeus Seneca

Selfishness isn't what they say it is.

In business, the American Management Association says that at work, you should always ask two questions when you interact with your co-workers: first, how do I get what I want, and, second, how do I keep the relationship? Very selfish questions, but if people stopped and asked those questions more often, there would be less conflict. In an attempt not to be seen as selfish, we paper over our selfish actions with allowable social labels, which fool no one.

It is critical to distinguish between "short" selfish, and "long" selfish. "Short" selfish is the immediate gratification of whatever you want this moment, regardless of the results. "Long" selfish is acting in accord with what you believe are your long term interests, considering probably results of actions. Both are condemned, but long selfish works.

Of course, selfish depends on your point of view. All those charming people out there trying to convert you to their particular faith gain at least a very warm feeling from their actions, which certainly could be construed as selfish. It is very common for them to be driven by their un-reconciled inner monsters, using your approval and conversion to help them hide another day, which is extremely selfish. But it is for a good cause, so it's okay.

Self-Destructiveness

Monsters are not self-destructive, despite the constant movies to the contrary. Movies have to end at some point, so they just get rid of the monster. Self-destructiveness is fearful, as it should be. But it is not fearful in the way we are taught. We are taught that self-destructiveness is indulging in vice. Go to sin, and sin will destroy you. (Sin, by the way, was a moon god, one of the most important Babylonian gods. "Going to Sin" was literally, at the time of the Old Testament, going to worship another god. It later developed a different meaning.)

Self-destructiveness is not just making oneself economically useless, which is what society is really concerned with. People drink, eat, drug themselves, and fool around all the time. It gets serious when you can't provide economic value to the system, as there are limited resources for supporting bad examples.

If you have completely bought into your official self, you will find yourself in a life that feels barren and devoid of interest. Your VISA can't buy enough meaningless things to fill the emptiness from destroying yourself, and then there are those monthly payments. The end of true self-destruction is an empty shell filled with fear, which crushes others to validate its nothingness. You don't want to be there, and you don't want to be near those lost people.

True self-destructiveness is destroying, wounding, and damaging parts of yourself. It is the destruction of your creativity, your ability to think, your personal freedom and hope. Yet those actions are not considered self-destructive by society. Quite the opposite: you are to function, you are to follow, you to be controlled by the group, and your hopes are narrowly defined and policed.

So are you self-destructive? That is a different question than "Are you destructive of your 'social' self (by being late, acting out, etc)? Do you play a virtue trap game? In that trap, there is always time for someone else, always time for another assigned task, always that effort, in every day and in every way, to be a better person. Isn't that complete obedience to your official person, and rather self-destructive?

You can be virtuous to a fault, which usually means you try too hard to achieve an ideal that was simply supposed to confuse you. Confused, frustrated at the contradictions in the virtues and your lack of time for yourself, you are trapped. Your true self, which didn't gain approval, which doesn't receive prime time, which society says there isn't any virtue in preserving, goes deep inside, and it's annoyed. It's not surprising that it pops up in dreams as a dark force.

Self-destructiveness is also an unwillingness to change because of other people. People put themselves in little boxes for safety: they may be unhappy, but they are safe. You open your box and it shakes theirs, and their fear of change is pushed on you. Then they are not happy, but they can take it out on you. People use the virtues as whips and the vices as scourges, so there you are, bleeding if you let them.

Safety is one of the most dangerous concepts out there. Safety is not standing in front of cars—we all agree on that. But is safety not rocking the boat socially, not thinking for yourself? That isn't safe for society, so certainly it shouldn't be safe for you. Safety doesn't really exist, however.

Let's be cheerful: you have been almost dead many times. Think about your near misses. What was your last one? What about the ones you didn't see? Each new life is an opportunity. Life is short. Each of us has regular "near misses," when you are almost killed in an accident of some kind. We calculate that about every six months, each of us experiences a near miss (cars are dangerous). It should be an opportunity to rethink/reevaluate—after all, you were almost dead, and the past is a sunken cost.

To digress, the concept of a sunken cost puzzles many people.

Things that happen in the past are done. OVER. Game ended, final buzzer sounded. If something in the past was a failure, then using today to put a false flow of success on the failure won't work. Money spent in a losing venture, time devoted to bad relationships—all this is just gone, and devoting today to justify the past actions loses today.

People wonder about what they would do if they got to start over. Being missed by a large truck is as close to starting over as you want to be. We all hear of people who change their lives when diagnosed with something awful, and the focus changes rapidly to the very short term. Why wait till then? Why not live now? Because it's risky to change.

Humans don't understand risk, really. The studies go on and on proving that we don't grasp risk. The actual problem is that we grasp risk in daily life in the Kalahari and surrounding areas in Africa, where our ancestors faced the challenges of daily life for eons. Those are not the same kind of risks we face today, and so Las Vegas and major insurance companies do quite well.

Because we have failed at things, because of the way our minds are hardwired, and most importantly, because society doesn't want us just running loose trying things, most of us are practiced at talking ourselves out of risk. We are skilled speculators on the probable pain of self-exposure, still acting out what are parents told us when we were four.

If you do something new, you will do it badly the first time—and probably the first few times. It isn't self-destructive to fail while try-ing. What is self-destructive is to fail to try. Trying and failing isn't failure: failure is failing to try. Kind of the same type of slogan as "no one plans to fail; they just fail to plan." We choose to set limits at the point where we feel assured of success. As time goes by, failures accu-mulate, and because we are not trying new things, successes dwindle. We may not be happy, but we feel safe. That is an illusion, and a very expensive one.

Many people react to their frustrations by trying to prove the world wrong. The world is what it is, and it really doesn't care. If you are focused on trying to live either up to a social reality or against that social reality, you will pay a price—it's just a matter of time.

But if you know yourself, you won't do self-destructive things. Monsters may be many things, but they are focused on survival. The destruction of monsters in movies and popular culture is more a function of the need for a plot line and making a moral lesson. One of the authors always wonders how many socially glowing, although structurally incoherent endings in TV and movies are part of a probation agreement imposed on the writers/producers/executives creating the movie/show/content.

Everyone loses sometimes, and often it's more important to have tried and lost than never to have tried. Don't bet black on the roulette table in Vegas over and over, though. That isn't a learning loss; that is pretending that your magical control over the universe can beat the law of probability. If you have that magical ability, use it on a big lottery jackpot. Otherwise, don't fool yourself.

When you have experienced a loss, you have to acknowledge it. "I lost" is painful. "I was robbed," "I was cheated," etc., is their fault. If you were robbed or cheated, learn something from that and move on. So you lost.

Why did you lose? Were you embarrassed? What dreams were stomped on? What dreams didn't you know you had until you became furious when they were stomped on? Pick up the dreams, and if they are good dreams, don't drop them. Learn what you can, reward yourself for trying, reward for yourself for understanding, and move on. Life has injuries. Your system is resilient, far tougher than you give yourself credit for.

And if the loss is a big one—the work is gone, the relationship is over, you are off the team—well, one door closes and another opens. Check with yourself; talk with your actual self, not the official self. Ask what's next and move on. If you only talk to the official self, then the same kind of losses will continue, because you don't know what you want to win.

Think about the model, the ideal you are following. It is so common for us to just grab a picture, a model from a movie or book, and try to follow that. This isn't new: Goethe wrote a book, *The Sorrows of Young Werther*, in 1772, which resulted in young men committing suicide for lost romance all over Europe. Perhaps it was a Darwinian weeding process, but don't just take models into you without thinking.

A large part of the problem of being human is that what we can handle intellectually far outstrips what we can handle emotionally. Just as every parent still sees his or her child in some ways as a four-year-old, regardless of the child's physical age, we are always four years old inside and very unhappy when something goes wrong, when someone is mad at us. Accept that four-year-old; listen to what he or she is saying. There is probably something useful in it – children do have a clarity of vision that adults carefully mask. But move on.

Of course, it's easier to say that than to do it. Each rejection is a blow to our view of ourselves. But those blows can only be finished by ourselves. The Buddhists have an example: an enemy shoots an arrow at you, which falls short at your feet. Do you pick up the arrow and shove it in your chest, finishing the enemy's plan, or do you walk away from the arrow and the pain.

Of course, if it was a Mongolian example, you would take the battle to the disarmed enemy and put the arrow through their heart, but that takes us down a different path. Sometimes it's better to walk away; sometimes you have to finish the battle. You do have to assess your enemy correctly: the Buddhist walking away from a Mongolian attack isn't going to live very long, as Mongol's don't walk away.

Outright hostility can be dealt with. It is not pleasant, but at least you know something about what the problem is. If you are short on outright hostility in your life, write a book and try to get it published: contact with agents/publishers will give you all the hostility you could ever desire. It is much more dangerous when you receive subtle, constant criticism that doesn't give anything positive back. If all you hear is the negative, then that's what you start thinking of. Acting against a negative doesn't create anything, because not doing a negative is a zero. Not accomplishing a negative isn't doing something. If you are focused on not being tense, that is something quite different from being relaxed. If you are focused on not losing, that is something very different than winning.

One of the authors recently attended a seminar where the speaker said you should control anger in the workplace, which certainly makes sense. They said don't just walk up to someone and shout about a problem. Walk up to the person, and in a calm, polite voice, say that there seems to be an issue to discuss. The speaker meant well, but from my experience, when someone does that, every alarm bell in your system should go off: they are armed and ready for the discussion, and you don't even know what is about to hit you. At least the angry person had not prepared an ambush.

If you let yourself be bullied by others into being nice or normal, then you have sold out. You lost. They may like your social face, but you will hate the social facade. If you hate yourself, you will lash out. You will eat too much, drink too much, your temper will explode. Then the losses really start adding up, and it's always *you* at that point: *you* are too angry, *you* are drinking too much. When you are acting out your frustration with someone else and letting that person pin the blame on you, there isn't any winning that game.

Therefore, self-destruction is far more than socially defined self-destruction. Committing socially defined self-destructive actions will destroy you, because there are some physically damaging choices there. But real self-destruction is following the unnecessary virtues that society pushes at you. Self-destruction is not finding and protecting yourself as a full person, beyond your usefulness as an economic entity.

Be positive. Don't see choices as walls or barriers; see them as hurdles and challenges. When you lose, immediately take one small action to support yourself. You are going to lose most of the time, which is the nature of life. The only true "losing" is not trying again. Don't make excuses to yourself why you don't have to try, why you failed, or worse yet, why you should have failed. We too often use excuses to avoid facing our fear.

I like the blues as a music art form, but it is a bad philosophy to live by. All that resignation and acceptance just isn't good for you. The goes same for country music. It's fun to listen to and great dancing music, but all that hard drinking and those bad choices—it's like running the plays from society's playbook completely backwards. Do that, and you will lose. You won't feel good losing, and you will know inside that you are living your life to prove something to someone else, which is an empty feeling.

The true self is a disturbing creature. It can be anarchistic, inconsistent by others standards, it knows how to play and how to say no to others while saying yes to yourself. Make wishes. Stop being an adult for a minute and throw a penny into a fountain, or create your own wishing station and use that mud puddle over there. Wishes are just wishes—they are frivolous—and that's why we should take them seriously, because the trivial allows us to express what is forbidden.

A path to self-destruction is to believe that work is work and not play. Anything that is fun isn't work. After all, that's why they pay you. We all say these things, and sometimes there are things you just have to do, but that doesn't mean you have to exult boredom and pain as some kind of necessary sacrifice. Don't think that doing what you like and are good at shouldn't be your work. No hair shirts—they don't work well in the washer anyhow. Don't think that what you want to do is frivolous and doesn't count in life.

Children are taught that God is a stern parent with very rigid ideas about what's appropriate for us, in other words, no fun. Society has invested a lot of time and effort in planting that idea really, really deep inside. You don't have to buy it. The creator is not the father/mother/church here on Earth who have beaten into us (non-violently, of course) their ideas of what is sensible for us. Children have an open mentality that absorbs information without requiring coherence. One of the key rules for a cult, if you are considering setting one up, is that the people be brought back to a childlike state of learning so they will absorb without question. You (and your inner monster) is key in this. You need to bring out those things just thrown into your mind as a child and integrate them into an adult system.

Do you equate difficulty with virtue, and creativity and enjoyment with fooling around? Perhaps you've heard, "Hard work is good," "It never killed anyone," etc. Something that comes to us easily and is fun must be some sort of trick, and it certainly won't pay a living wage. So as you get older, you do less and less of the things you enjoy. You tell yourself, and others, that life is doing what you must do. It doesn't work. The center won't hold. You don't believe it inside. The doing is bogged down, and not done as well, and your workplace is happy to retire you when they can because you are frozen up inside—and outside.

> "If you tell a lie big enough and keep repeating it, people will eventually come to believe it. The lie can be maintained only for such time as the State can shield the people from the political, economic and/ or military consequences of the lie. It thus becomes vitally important for the State to use all of its powers to repress dissent, for the truth is the mortal enemy of the lie, and thus by extension, the truth is the greatest enemy of the State."
>
> —Dr. Joseph Goebbels,
> Reich Minister of
> Public Enlightenment
> and Propaganda

You wouldn't live your life according to his principles, such as they were. Why do you tell yourself lies over and over until you believe them? Why reject the truth?

CHAPTER 13: MONSTERS ARE...

Monsters Are the Bad

Monsters are defined by society as the bad. They are something to use as a clear "THIS IS BAD" sign. Society defines monsters as that which they are afraid of, which is, most critically, people not doing what they are supposed to do when they are supposed to do it. That is why monsters are cast into the dark view, because : even if you are not afraid of monsters, society is afraid.

This, perversely, is very helpful in feeding your inner monster, because you are then looking at what they don't want you to look at, what society finds so horrible in trying to control people that they have done everything they can to fence that area off. What society finds horrible is you: your free thought, your internal strength, and your ability to choose.

Surprisingly, monsters are attributed with some important strengths, which makes you wonder what society has in mind by driving those strengths to the outside. Monsters are typically physically and mentally tough, so that defeating the monsters in stories is difficult. Monsters are resourceful; they keep coming back and back, in new shapes and with new plans. And they are certainly focused; the goals that the monsters seek are by definition outside the pale, but they are absolutely focused on those goals.

Monsters are always shown doing something and saying something – in the first place, you need dialog. Even growls and roars say something, namely that the monster is outside the group. More importantly, the juxtaposition of a set of unrelated actions and words puts the words and concepts outside the accepted, without further thought. So if the monster is rending people apart and saying something, then the something said is assumed to be tied to the rending, which isn't always necessarily correct.

Monsters are un-socialized, elemental forces – they do as they want, answer to themselves.

A monster acts for itself. What could be more threatening to society than those things? A monster is an unsocialized creature. There is nothing that society hates more than a creature that doesn't play by the society's rules, a creature that plays by the creature's rules.

A monster is an elemental force that acts by its own laws, according to its own nature. Gravity, electro-mechanical forces, are what they are. Don't defy the law of gravity without a parachute, and don't defy that vast bulk rearing out of the water; leave as quietly as you can.

Monsters are life; they are organic creatures, full of senses, feelings, emotions, and experiences. Those kinds of feelings are hard to control at the society level, so they are pushed down, pushed out into the dark.

Legend had it that at the edge of the medieval mariner's map was written, "Beyond this point lie monsters." "Monsters" was shorthand for "Don't go there, idiot," and it worked better, because the best way to get a human to do something is to tell them not to. Monsters on the other hand, have teeth and difficult dispositions, and were reputed to eat people, so people might avoid those.

Times and views change, and so do the monsters thrown at us. A lot of the behavior in the Old Testament would be considered monstrous today. Many clerics grimace at reconciling those stories with today's softer messages. The Old Testament people lived in harder times than ours and faced very hard decisions. The kind of mellow pap that passes for spiritual guidance today is unsuitable for truly difficult situations. Difficult isn't choosing between options that are less than ideal; difficult is when the group's survival depends on actions far outside the pale.

As the good varies from culture to culture, monstrous actions vary. Eating pork is accepted in many places and abhorred as unholy in many others. The stigma against left handedness, partly arising from the distrust of the different, seems to have been rooted in very real personal cleanliness issues that exist in many cultures even today. Don't eat dog in the United States, but they are a delicacy in Asia.

Monsters Protect Themselves

Monsters protect themselves: monsters are very good at the rough stuff, and the rough stuff inside is harder than the rough stuff outside.

Part of what society hates about monsters is that they watch out for themselves; they just don't "assume the position" when society barks. Monsters protect themselves – they know they are all they have got. To protect yourself, you have to be good at the rough stuff, which is a lot more than physical combat.

In reality, anytime you have to engage in physical combat you have already lost. *The Art of War* says,

> "Therefore, one hundred victories in one hundred battles is not the most skillful. Subduing the other's military without battle is the most skillful."[24]

And the same advice goes for verbal or other combat. Television and the movies glorify combat and conflict, but they rig the game before they play. The net result is a morality show, with the play set to make the point that society always wins. The real rough stuff, therefore, is thinking about what is thrown at you. External action takes place within the social sphere, but monsters define that external action by their thought, not by parroting back behavior.

A constant refrain in this book is that your monster takes you to the places you need to be to see yourself. Those are the places you have been ignoring, because society doesn't want you to look there. They are not allowed to be thought about, since they will raise problems.

In the real world, the people who act against your interests are in camouflage—they operate in the light under the banner of the "right." And there are real monsters stalking out there who don't operate alone. As easy as it is to blame to Hitler, Stalin, Pol Pot, and other fearless leaders, they just issue orders; others do the work, and they seem surprisingly happy to do it.

Monsters Are Organic—And So Are We

Organic is a horror for people. All those messy structures and curving lines, uncontrollable behaviors, terrible urges and aberrant appearances. Things that look like they came from deep in the sea,

---

[24] Sun Tzu, *The Art of War*, ibid.

things that don't look like you and me. Monsters are organic because people reject the organic, life at its basic messy nature. This is partly hard wired, partly trained. While we all like a limited subset of the real world, cute is the criteria for what we like. The nasty, the decay process and its odd shaped actors, are feared and detested.

Monsters are typically oddly shaped masses of tissue, leaking fluids from body parts better hidden. (An exception is the movie *V for Vendetta*. Who were the monsters in that movie? They certainly were not the person in the mask)

Monsters are all the sensory feelings we are trained to push away—sensual pleasures (can't you feel the sin finders rising up at the words?), pleasures of the flesh (now all the sin finders are on duty). Given the elaborate design and range of pleasure receptors, wouldn't you say they were put there to be used?

Our ancestors lived (granted, not as long as we do) under sanitary conditions better not thought of. You can see why the catchy slogan "Cleanliness is next to godliness" and the like were so necessary to change habits, when you look how people used to live.

Monsters typically flourish in awful sanitary conditions, which is part of the "bad" message. And there are many reasons why clean is better, for example, disease doesn't flourish as well. But like most things, people take this too far. Try to eliminate all dirt, and you end up with kids with asthma. Try to eliminate all bacteria, and you will kill off the bacteria that ensure your daily survival. Moderate exposure to germs and dirt strengthens the system, which seems counter to what generations of mothers fought against.

The following quote demonstrates our rejection of our organic nature:

> "*Inter faeces et urinam nascimur* (Man is born between feces and urine)."
>
> —Saint Augustine

And so being a human is awful because of where they start. It also has the effect of neatly putting women on an even lower rung at the same time.

Where else would the birth process occur? Where else is there prime real estate on the human body for the relatively rare act of reproduction (not thinking, actually doing)? Perhaps out the belly button, with a zipper or Velcro?

And yes, urine and feces do smell, but they are waste products – good smelling waste products are a bad thing, as ingestion of waste products has a detrimental effect on human health. Villages that have the toilet facilities upstream of the drinking water do not last long, so the bad smell is an important message. Further proof of this is the multitude of packaged sugar treats we have today that taste great and don't seem to do much of anything positive. Type II diabetes with those chips, anyone?

Monsters, when we look at how they appear, generally seem weak on personal grooming, they smell bad, (hard to tell in movies, but we don't see a lot of monster showers) and they ooze things we don't want to think about. It is somewhat ironic, but typical, that the new focus on 'organic' tends to be of the kitten-cute variety, not the ugly bugs.

Being organic means emitting things that the senses can catch. That is actually what the senses were designed for. For example, many species emit odor pheromones (sexual attractants), and there are continued arguments about whether humans also emit them. If they exist, the first person to isolate and manufacture them will make a substantial amount of money, if the manufacture isn't immediately banned (in which case they will make ten times that much in the black market).

If you look at the way that dogs, cats, and other animals with far better sense of smell than ours check each other, it makes you wonder about our obsession with grooming. Not that lack of grooming seems to change anything – our ancestors, who would bathe perhaps once a year, cheerfully seem to have reproduced like rabbits. And perhaps that is the root of our obsession, because recognizing the organic and responding to smell cues at the church dance would surely violate at least several major virtues. It might even get you in the newspaper.

Not that we're objecting, because unwashed people in grocery stores certainly cut one's appetite, and some things about socialization we cannot praise too much. The point is that we are completely (in a practical, operating sense) organic. Denying that nature means you start a long way from what you really are.

Perhaps it is that mass of contradictions that makes humans the daily joy they are. Plato, with his concept of the pure beauty of the idea, clearly rejects all that is organic as low and disgusting. Given the technology for sewage disposal in his time, it was probably a pretty easy call. As an ideological approach to life, this isn't just incorrect; it is damaging, because you are not paying attention to what is but rather how you want it to be, a very dangerous thing when the "want to be" doesn't have any relationship to the real world.

There are more cells in your body without your DNA than with your DNA. We are actually colony creatures, yet many people are horrified of bugs. Some of the bugs are bad, but without a lot of bugs in your body you would be dead in a few seconds. Those bugs keep us alive (and themselves to, a good system) from moment to moment.

Dogs and other animals are not that different from us. If you watch a dog chase a Frisbee or a ball, the dog looks at the object when it takes flight and projects a trajectory in its mind. Watch the dog take off, looking at where it expects the ball to go, and while in flight the ball hits a tree midway. The dog goes to where the ball should be and then looks back. That is the exact same behavior you would follow trying to catch a ball or other object, and the dog is just as annoyed as you would be.

. Nature tends to be conservative and economical about behaviors, and when it finds one that works, it sticks with it. The process of tracking movement and tracking events (like balls, sticks, or other flying objects) in the real world is probably much the same essential computer sub model in animals as in humans.

For good or bad, humans are far less original than the myths have made us out to be. The sad thing is that the myths, by making the greatness of humans dependent on the smallness of the other creatures, and by rejecting our organic nature, has lost the incredible wonder of the process of life. We overlook the wonder of the complexity of the life process because it is there and wallow in the daily trivia that seems new. We worship what seem like esoteric things that are tinker toys compared to the complexity of life. But I digress.

Really, the key difference between humans and all other species is that we accumulate knowledge. If dogs could communicate knowledge to each other, then the tenth generation would be considerably different from the first. For whatever combination of reasons—opposable thumbs, brain construction, speech, an environment that allows for physical accumulation of knowledge (dolphins may be smart but what would you write on underwater – and what would you write with?) humans have a tremendous ability to change the physical world.

So we are not completely different from everything around us. The actual DNA is very much the same. If you doubt how organic we are, think about the last time you made a conscious decision to do something that your digestive system disagreed strongly with. We can promise you can't beat your digestive system, and it has very clear and organic ways of showing its displeasure.

What discussion of the organic would be complete without sex? Not looking at sex, because then there are pictures and publishing problems, as well as a considerable loss of focus, so let's just think about the issue.

Sex is as organic as it gets—all touch, feel, smells and dripping liquids. Then there are actual hidden entrances into the body, and projections out from the body, which change the social and public presentation of each of us. How monstrous is that! There was a weird cartoon I saw once showing orifice buildings, with strangely shaped and placed openings. Why are pictures of these prohibited, even though each human carries one of the banned objects with them all the time?

The orifices and projections, by placement and linked functions, are tied to the excretory functions so condemned by philosophers. Actually, it could be worse. The platypus is a descendent of a line of mammals with a combined orifice for defecation, urination, and reproduction—we have tremendously sophisticated hardware in comparison to that.

A *lot* of the socially defined virtues are focused on sex. Those that are not tied to the actions are tied to the relations (technically the lack of physical relations) between the two sexes. The absolute brilliance of the system is that the virtues enforcement in the modern world is by the females.

This is considerably different from enforcement in traditional societies. Sexual virtue in tribal areas in Pakistan, for example, clearly are controlled by the males in very direct and physical ways. One would guess that the females have a control set of rules within female groups, but it's certainly less visible. That underlying economic structure is still the basic agrarian model of the past five thousand years, with its lack of importance of the individual and the overriding control of the group.

The African system of female genital mutilation seems designed to minimize female sexual activity by making it painful and difficult. It may make the village function better, but the cost to the individuals is astonishingly high. If that isn't a monstrous behavior, it is isn't clear what would be.

This is a good example of a system as simply an accretion of behaviors from the past. How that system of genital mutilation developed is unknown, but it is now part of the system, and it can hardly be challenged in many places because that is the "right." One can only imagine the reaction in the media to an isolated individual mutilating a few women's genitals, but when it is society wide, it's just what they do. Within those social groups, attacking the practice is considered monstrous, a rejection of the sacred virtues from the forefathers.

Do monsters have sex? Well, they have to come from somewhere, and that's how life starts. In the *Lord of the Rings* series, the orcs somehow came directly out of the earth, but that was a really incoherent solution. If that is where orcs came from, then we would literally be up to our armpits in orcs, and people wouldn't stand a chance.

Certainly the sex act is considered monstrous by many of society's structures, and banned by common mores. We find it amusing to talk to young couples who say that they are working on having children. They are married, they have jumped through all the legal and ethical hoops, and they are "working" on children? It sounds so painful. Isn't this the same set of actions that was fun while dating?

Monsters Disrupt

Monsters are disruptors. They cause change and are the forerunners of change. Monsters uproot our daily patterns and the town layout. If they were dependable, they could bid on demolition work, but they are probably non-union.

Monsters make us look at what is, not what we want or prefer.

Because of the disruption, the change, a monster is going to be the dark side. That only makes sense. As discussed repeatedly, the social structures load the choices; the "good" is defined by their goals. For example, the "good" were the socialist heroes who worked themselves to death for the greater happiness of the proletariat, a standard trope in State-approved plays and movies. Curiously enough, only commissars got the villas, not the families of the heroic (but deceased) workers.

Disruption is traditionally a social disaster. Farmers tend to be very conservative people, because changes can have expected consequences when it is too late to fix them. Disruption can damage the harvest. No harvest, no village. So disruption is at the heart of what society traditionally didn't want. In today's world, disruption is our hope for the future, so we need to think like monsters and around corners.

What Is a Monster?

Given that the chapter started with "Monsters Are…" aren't we a little slow getting to this definition? Well, there is a lot more to monsters than just their physical appearance, or what is thrown at us. Hopefully you agree after wading this far into the chapter.

What comes to mind when you think of a monster? They come in all sizes, shapes, and types. There are,

Alien monsters
Swamp monsters
The dark, the shape in the fog
The noise where there shouldn't be
Diseased, dead, and decaying monsters
Things that look like the bugs under a rock, but bigger
Social monsters, who look just like you
Perverted monsters, the mainstay of the mass media

Monsters can be organized by characteristics.

Physical characteristics: What are their sizes, shapes, and exteriors?

Mental characteristics: How do they think? What is different about a monsters thinking, and what different mental abilities does the monster have? Do they think iIllogically, dangerously, or rationally in a way that isn't approved? Can they read minds, move things with their mind, control machinery?

Spiritual characteristics: Do they follow different goals, deny and/or think about the social virtues, and encourage people to think and not blindly follow the system? By social standards, those monsters may be crippled and warped.

Social characteristics: Do they defy the established order? Each culture and country has its social monsters. In India, caste jumping (at least in the past, and in the present in many cases) showed no regard for the established order in the system. Not long ago in the United States, non-whites who sought professional positions were monsters. In ancient Japan, in as tightly knit a social structure as could be created, there were clear rules for the farmers, merchants, and lords. Social monsters who challenged those fared poorly.

What do you see when you think "monster"? When you hear the word "monster," what picture do you have? If you have a piece of paper, rapidly drawn the outlines, in an inexpert and rough-hand way. Don't show the drawing to anyone; put it aside.

If you are a productive economic entity in the cubical mazes, then isn't that a parody of the *Living Dead* movies (since the dead come to life at 5:00 p.m.)?

Where are monsters found?

Under stairs?
Under bridges?
In closets?
Under the bed?
In the dark?
In the cubicle next to you?

Then there are the monsters in the culture and entertainment. The list of monsters in movies, with pictures and dialogue, would be far larger than this book: Frankenstein's monster, Godzilla, Freddy, Michael Myers, Alien—a huge range of creatures and humanoids. It would be a fun book, with a lot more pictures. So, monsters are everywhere in popular culture.

What do monsters do?

- Scaring kids.

- Lurking in the dark.

- Bumping in the night

Monsters are and do what the powers that be decree is wrong. Images of the sick, of decay, disproportion and death are tied to the thoughts and actions that society fears, so that the thoughts and actions can't even be considered.

In the movies and books, being a monster isn't a bad experience—at least until the final denouncement, when for plot and publishing reasons the monster gets it. Look at Senator (later Emperor) Palpatine, the only person in *Star Wars* who seems to be enjoying himself the entire time. In *Paradise Lost*, a common quiet complaint against the book is that Lucifer gets all the best lines. Can you think of other happy monsters?

PART III: FINDING AND FEEDING YOUR INNER MONSTER

Chapter 14: Monsters Can…

You need to be able, at any time call an image to your mind for strength and power. Not an image that diverts you from where you are at, but an image that focuses you now on what you are facing.

You need this when it's tough, when lots of things are happening at once. I prefer the following poem:

If you can keep your head when all about you
Are losing theirs and blaming it on you,
If you can trust yourself when all men doubt you
But make allowance for their doubting too,
If you can wait and not be tired by waiting,
Or being lied about, don't deal in lies,
Or being hated, don't give way to hating,
And yet don't look too good, nor talk too wise;

If you can dream-and not make dreams your master,
If you can think-and not make thoughts your aim;
If you can meet with Triumph and Disaster
And treat those two imposters just the same;
If you can bear to hear the truth you've spoken
Twisted by knaves to make a trap for fools,
Or watch the things you gave you life to, broken,
And stoop and build 'em up with worn-out tools;

If you can make one heap of all your winnings
And risk it all on one turn of pitch-and-toss,
And lose, and start again at your beginnings
And never breath a word about your loss;

If you can force your heart and nerve, and sinew
To serve your turn long after they are gone,
And so hold on when there is nothing in you
Except the Will which says to them: "Hold on!"

If you can talk with crowds and keep your virtue,
Or walk with kings-nor lose the common touch,
If neither foes nor loving friends can hurt you;
If all men count with you, but none too much,
If you can fill the unforgiving minute
With sixty seconds' worth of distance run
Yours is the Earth and everything that's in it,
And-which is more-you'll be a Man, my son!

—Rudyard Kipling

And let's not be sexist-let's take "man" as generic human, not limited to males. Kipling is today dismissed because of his militant willingness to stand up. There isn't any victimization in that poem; there are no excuses, no apologies. There is merely the willingness to be what you can be in an uncertain and often disagreeable world. The goal of this book is to give you tools to do what he describes in that poem.

You want to call your focus to your aid, not spend your efforts pushing things away, like fear. Your inner monster is you becoming a person, not another's idea of a useful economic actor. No one else is going to push that power button for you or train you to use it when you need it. Perhaps the army can train you to use a button when they need it, but outside that structure, you are on your own.

The world requires constant decisions based on incomplete information and an uncertain future. The official self is reactive to risk. Being reactive means selecting from the choices presented to you. Being proactive means making up those choices yourself, but you have to reach your actual self, your plans to be proactive.

Images handed to you by others are powered by them, and you have to pay for their use. When it's happening, you don't have time for rituals to call power to you. There isn't any time to invoke a complex set of negotiations. You can't call someone to hold your hand as they chant their position.

And whatever creator you worship, what would have been the point of creating autonomous (definition: not controlled by others or by outside forces; existing and functioning independently) creatures who can't help themselves? You were given all these abilities. Use them.

This Is the Critical Dividing Point in the Book

Up to this point, we have looked at how society defines the good for itself. In that defining, society overreaches and over controls, and what is thrown out as the bad is the best parts of ourselves.

After this chapter, the book is focused on finding and feeding your inner monster. Your inner monster can bring you to yourself and bring coherence to yourself.

We Fear but Love Monsters

We are fascinated by monsters because our conscious/unconscious mind recognizes the freedom monsters have.

Your inner monster can be freedom, but only for people with something inside. If there isn't anyone inside, then this is not your book.

> "The dogmas of the quiet past are inadequate to the stormy present. The occasion is piled high with difficulty, and we must rise with the occasion. As our case is new, so we must think anew and act anew."
>
> —Abraham Lincoln

Monsters always have power outside normal human abilities. Sometimes the power is to think or act outside the rules. Often the power is physical, mental, spiritual, or a combination of these traits. Generally the monster has an organic physical appearance or can manifest things that are "too organic" for people to deal with. While there is a huge variation in monsters, they all have something outside the normal view. You of course don't choose just any monster—you instead focus on the monster that is you, that brings out your abilities and strengths that you have denied. Your inner monster can then bring you,

Strength, Toughness, Power

Monsters don't run; monsters don't wimp out or bow to whatever social grace there is. Your monster rises within you, able to stand and encourage you through hard times. Your inner monster isn't dependent on your ability to meet a certain set of social graces. Your inner monster is your inner monster – you don't have to go through a magic set of actions for it to be on your side.

> "If we are to achieve results never before accomplished, we must expect to employ methods never before attempted."
>
> —Francis Bacon

Social Structures Can't Guarantee Strength

Social posing/posturing—gaining the agreement of whatever small group is most important to you on a daily basis—isn't going to give you real strength, toughness, or power. For one thing, you have to go back to the group, and their interests are necessarily different from yours, especially when trouble is here.

Secondly, in the rare case that the group's interests are the same as yours, you have to act from the inside, which is different from the people standing next to you saying you can do it. They usually are not there at the right time, anyhow.

Finally, social posing is a virulent variant of social reality, and just because your sub group says this works, that often bears very little relationship to what works in the larger world. You know this somewhere inside, but it can be squashed down. This isn't just in the 'hood. Ask the people who used to work for Arthur Andersen, a highly respected conservative firm, a mainstay of the system, which went right off a cliff when top management focused on money and forgot integrity.

The institutions that endorse and frame society, the churches and the like, will often not be effective figures for you to rely on. They have a system and need payment, either in money or spirit. Don't expect them to patronize you without wanting to be paid something additional for it. Like your health insurance company, which is careful to write insurance that won't be required: don't have an existing condition if you want their help! The gold certainly does rule.

The social structure will reject you at times, even when there was an implicit promise it would support you. How many times have you seen or heard of people falsely accused while doing the right thing, only to discover that they are *way* outside – just kidding about wanting people to take those positions. Energy is a constant in the universe, and it's the same with society—people will maintain the same degree of disdain and anger; they just move from target to target, shooting the one in front of them, right or wrong.

The structure will turn on you in large ways and small. Your inner monster is the key to avoid merely jumping to another structure, which usually makes things worse, or bowing down before the structure placed before you.

The persistence of form long after substance is gone is like a dead tree that people still see as living and use for structure. As they lean on it, they ignore that it is rotting, to their own peril. The ability of humans to rationalize that they are owed, were wronged, or whatever it takes to justify themselves, is all it takes to continue down a useless path – if one's peer group signs up also.

Your inner monster doesn't want a fake life; it wants to live. Your inner monster often isn't going to mesh well with your peer group, especially if your life is a mass of contradictions that are wearing you out. This is as true for the churchgoing social stalwart as it is for the pariah.

Monsters are good at stepping outside–that's what monsters do, in the end. The role models you are handed are not outside, and without your inner monster, you are stuck in the Jedi trap—forever afraid of the dark, afraid to step near it. Knowing the dark is going to know what lies waiting in the dark, and it's a lot better to know what is out there than to have it step into your parlor one day as a surprise.

Make the monster fun and enjoyable to yourself—it is your monster, and your strength. Out of nowhere, you will suddenly see that you are starting to look at things differently, taking different steps that are what you want, almost besides yourself. Months after discovering some ideas, some feelings, they will start to sparkle and be useful in ways not anticipated.

Monsters accept selfishness; they realize where selfish interest lies and where they want go for it. Selfishness is good and can result in real good in the world. What you do for a selfish wish to be accepted or other personal needs means you thought about what you want and what is needed to accomplish your goal. It doesn't mean just forcing the result you want, what people typically think of as selfish.

Difficult Times Require Internal Toughness

Sometimes you have to be ready and able to do a Godzilla. You have to able to stand up in your mind and walk across that hostile landscape.

You need your inner monster if you are having job problems or interpersonal problems. Job problems usually multiply into a whole gamut of problems: destroyed daily routine, debt (creditors!), and damaged interpersonal relationships go south. You lose a job, and it's like social leprosy. People flee the sick because they may catch it too, or they are reminded of how close to the edge they are. Problems seem to grow like the Hydra, where you cut off one head and two grow back.

Where people are waving social markers, and you are unsure, confused, uncertain, and unmoored, you just need that raw, focused anger inside to keep going. Remember that you are always committing at least one of the mortal sins, if by doing nothing else than reading this book, which is a sign of your dissatisfaction. (Bad peasant) This doesn't mean you have to externalize. The typically defined externalization is completely within the social flags—don't fall for it. But it does mean you have to have the fight, the ability, and the anger to keep your head up and keep on your path.

So your inner monster acts for you, cares about you, and doesn't buy the nonsense. What can be darker, in a real-world drama, than the social institutions setting you up to fail and then beating you down for your failure? If you don't know the dark within, how can you know others and realize what they are capable of? How can you know yourself, know your strength?

Your monster can help you trust your vision and choices. And, eventually, you are going to do what you want to do on the inside. Why not know about it rather than be surprised along with everyone else?

What the first part of the book has argued is that the social structure doesn't deal in good faith. Values and markers are laid out not as guides to a happier life for you but as control mechanisms. You are intentionally wrapped in a web, bound by contradictory strings so that in your confusion, "they" can provide answers. Where you respect certain people, you may seek their answers, but the training (indoctrination, actually) we all receive allows all kinds of people with all kinds of motives to pull on those strings. If you don't listen, they let the spider get you. If you face the spider, they can do nothing to you.

Almost all novels are based on a conflict between the official self and the actual self: generally a rather sudden collision with the actual self. Fiction is fun to read, but you don't want to be in that play. You want to know your actual self, which is what your inner monster brings.

> "Look well into thyself; there is a source of strength which will always spring up if thou wilt always look there."
>
> —Marcus Aurelius Antoninus,
> Roman emperor, A.D. 161–180

119

CHAPTER 15: FINDING YOUR INNER MONSTER

> "The individual has always had to struggle to keep from being overwhelmed by the tribe. If you try it, you will be lonely often, and sometimes frightened. But no price is too high to pay for the privilege of owning yourself."
>
> —Friedrich Nietzsche

This is not a "rational" process. Remember that German philosophy discussion of why words are inadequate in the "concepts" chapter? We are seeking communication with the non-verbal portions of yourself. The idea is to just let go and imagine: it's the unexpected you are after. You are moving to a different thinking and understanding of yourself, and thus the world around you.

Finding and feeding your inner monster is the rather indirect and inexact process of connecting with the non-verbal parts of yourself. As "you" are the bad, "you" have been pushed away and rejected. Those parts of you are still there, full of energy and power, but you have been trained to run from them. They are inner monsters, not because they are dangerous or destructive to you, but because society considers them possibly dangerous to it, and in any event unnecessary for society's purposes.

The book can only give advice; you have to open to yourself alone. Advice, even the best intended, is difficult to give and receive.

> "Thinking is easy, acting is difficult, and to put one's thoughts into action is the most difficult thing in the world."
>
> —Johann Wolfgang Goethe

The problem with seeking advice is that when you tell someone your problem, they do not know all about you. How then can another choose better than you? You can't even tell yourself all about yourself, because many of the most important things about you are bubbling just below consciousness, but they are no less important because of that. Recent brain research has found that a few seconds before you consciously decide to do something, the brain scan shows activity, and the decision had been made; the body moves into action before the thought even reaches your consciousness.[25]

It is even more complex than that: brain research on people who have had the connection between the right brain and left brain severed discovered some conceptually explosive results. Researchers could trigger an action by one side of the brain, and the other side of the brain could give a rational, logical reason for the action. The explanation was, of course, completely wrong, because there was no communication between the part of the brain acting and the part explaining. But to the people making the explanation, their explanation was the answer to why they had done what they had done. While the observer knew their response was objectively false, the person believed what they said.

Obviously, that makes a person a little leery as to whether rationally verbalizing your alternatives and choices is an accurate way to discover anything about you. It does show, by presenting a socially allowable justification, something about what you value presenting to the world and yourself. It makes absolutely clear the necessity to communicate with your non-verbal self, to feel and experience more than the thin veneer that consciousness presents.

Finding your inner monster is not about "visions" or different personalities. Actually, quite the opposite. The creatures of the horror world are our internal fears, made gooey and fearful in the flesh. Those fears are the "bad you" that society has defined and carefully trained. Humans are visual beings. A visual image connects with all the parts of the brain. You are putting images to the rejected actual self to bring yourself into coherence, and out of the confusion and chaos that the social structure prefers.

The social self is an actor in a play in your mind, with the plot and dialogue written by your first-grade teacher, your prior minister, your college roommate, your spouse, your mother-in-law, the movie

---

[25] neuroscientist John-Dylan Haynes at the Bernstein Center for Computational Neuroscience in Berlin, who is pioneering this research.

you saw when you were fourteen, and the book you read last week, mixed with all of flotsam and jetsam accumulated over life. The social self spouts to itself, like Hamlet talking to the skull, trying to justify and defend to an audience in your mind whatever random event it encounters. Isn't that rather mad? That is the model of socially rational behavior?

You are already a monster. Distasteful as it may seem, you are actually a colony creature—a mass of various cellular entities, a significant portion with different DNA. A lumbering, organic assembly of oozing fluids and ravenous appetites. All these creatures function in one skin, and your brain is an amazing collection of bits and pieces, computer routines and subroutines in today's view, accumulated over eons of evolution.

Technically, we are mobile bags of sea water—it doesn't get any more organic that that. We are monsters with a social façade when needed, and we shove ourselves away to play nice.

Actually, seeing ourselves as we are and not comparing ourselves to others is humility, a traditional virtue.

> "Men go abroad to wonder at the heights of mountains, at the huge waves of the sea, at the long courses of the rivers, at the vast compass of the ocean, at the circular motions of the stars, and they pass by themselves without wondering."
>
> —St. Augustine

Opening yourself to fantasy about different views of the world and yourself won't hurt anything. You have to view yourself in different ways before you can really see yourself. It's like walking around a house—you can imagine what the side and back look like, but you don't really know until you go there. While the sides may bear some relationship to the front that you show, the back can be completely different. Shouldn't you know that?

What do you need in your life? What would you want, if you had ability to wish and not just for money, which is a crutch to purchase something? What inside are you trying to purchase, what is the end result that wealth, etc. would bring to you? If you had the proverbial three wishes from a genie, what would you wish for? And no cheating, no asking for additional wishes.

What would you do if you didn't need to work/go to school/present daily routine? Would you sleep more? Would you have people to cook, clean, garden, and clear the snow? Those are all wishes for more time for you to do something else. What would you do that extra time? When your official self or the community says what you should do with your time, where do you look in yourself to see what you want?

Finding your inner monster isn't going to be like *Fight Club*, where the hero had a completely separate personality that went around without him knowing it. That is actually the opposite of what we are after here. In that movie, what he wanted was so far buried that it just took over occasionally rather than discuss the matter. We want to bring that monster in, we want the strength that comes from having a unified self.

What would you do if you knew you could not fail? What kind of monster would mean you would not fail?

What are you afraid of? What kind of monster is bothering you? What do you need to combat it?

> "I know well what I am fleeing from but not what I am in search of."
>
> —Michel de Montaigne

Do you deny the darkness within? Does the darkness bother you? Do you think the darkness is dis-ease? Dis-comfort? You are right—the darkness is you, shouting out to your official self. You can't really be at ease, you can't really be comfortable, until you embrace that dark as yourself.

Before you accept your inner monster, you are dis-eased, because you are:

- Angry
- Dissatisfied

123

- Dulled

- Depressed

- Drugged

Tell yourself of the darkness within, and the night will be afraid of you.

Imaginary Playmates

Let's start at a simple level. How many of us (no need to show hands) had imaginary playmates? They are actually an important socialization device, allowing a person to practice certain kinds of events in your mind before trying them out. But imaginary playmates are discouraged for many reasons.

First, imaginary playmates can easily be considered a sign of classic madness. The clear evidence is that the symptoms of classical madness—visions, voices, etc., are just hard wired into our brains. Some unfortunate (perhaps fortunate, if they work for them) people just have brain chemistry and/or wiring that works differently. I remember reading an article about a person who saw visions. After relaxation therapy, she still saw them, but she wasn't worried by them, which had to be progress. However, the visions didn't go away; her brain chemistry just worked like that.

Just like physical illness, mental illness is a biological event. So exploring monsters and alternative views of the world won't make biological changes in you. You can't grow an extra arm, even if you think about it really hard for a long time. You can't even enlarge parts of your body that you might want to. You are not going to re-hardwire your brain by thought. The neural pathways will change with time, but the size and functioning of the various components of the brain are genetically determined.

One of the nice things about today's world is that you can happily walk down the street, talking and gesturing wildly, and as long as you have your Bluetooth receiver on your ear, you are good. It helps if you are actually carrying on a phone conversation with someone, but that is another issue.

Like religious concepts that were developed for one purpose and morphed into different uses, there are "science" terms describing mental states—psychotic, neurotic, personality disorder—and the permutations run for thousands of pages. In clinical settings, the terms are more or less defined and perform useful functions. Pulled outside those settings, the terms can be thrown around as command-and-control devices. Because they are "science," we are trained to bow to them.

Again, true mental problems, like physical problems, are physically based. Using the science terms outside those physically based problems just muddies the water. When the terms are applied to daily functioning, the terms become meaningless.

In the movie *Airplane II!*, a patient at a mental hospital is raving that he won't pay $2,000 a day for hostile nurses, incompetent doctors, inedible food, and terrible physical surroundings. A passing doctor casually dismisses the man as "crazy," when it is pretty obvious the man is expressing rational concerns.

The inner monsters we are seeking can be shoved aside as neuroses and personality problems, because finding the actual self is a problem for the structure. Opening yourself to the dark within is actually what therapists are for, although that can be a rather expensive step. The professions/priesthood carry their own ideological baggage with them. Visualize your inner monsters, make yourself coherent, and you will save thousands of dollars (and time commuting to the appointments).

The real problem with imaginary playmates is that they diminish the importance of the social structure. Your imaginary playmates can function as an alternative source of strength and pleasure, and the socialization system can't have that. You have to buy into the rewards and punishments of the system so that the system can persuade you to do the frequently boring and sometimes disgusting things that make daily life function.

In many ways, adulthood is vastly overrated. While it is nice to have money and some personal freedom, being a responsible adult involves a lot of what used to be called sacrifice. When you have two children, a mortgage, and two car loans, the money is gone and personal freedom is rather illusory. Now, the rewards of children and a home cannot be expressed in dollars, which is the *new*—you don't ever get what you wanted, but sometimes you get more. And when the children are teenagers, you get a lot more than you wanted.

Acting responsibly is more than drinking in moderation, which is something you owe yourself—why destroy your liver? Responsibility is handling the really unpleasant things that pop up in family and personal relationships that you really would rather just let go of. Don't you wonder why people can't solve their own problems? And why do they want others to participate in their losing games with them? If you are asking those questions a lot, then you are letting others define your choices and time for you. Being responsible sometimes means making others responsible for themselves.

An easy way into this process is to go back to imaginary play-mates. As you get older, you begin to think that the imaginary friends were not so bad after all—at least they don't hire lawyers when they get mad. If you have to talk to someone, talk to your dog, who will follow in rapt fascination, impressed by your cleverness and depth of thought. Don't talk to your cat, because they disdain everything.

But this imaginary playmate comes from the social outside. The outside is where you are taught not to go, and much of the information thrown at us about monsters is just random counterpoint; it isn't coherent and complete. The process of moving to the outside and seeing new things brings knowledge. Considered and accumulated knowledge brings wisdom.

> "The greatest explorer on this earth never takes voy-
> ages as long as those of the man who descends to the
> depth of his heart."
>
> —Julien Green

Today, you have opportunities that your ancestors never dreamed of. The economic structure allows you to function as more than a tool to get the harvest in. The economic structure wants you to think, to define your own work and make choices. Again, it wasn't long ago (and for huge parts of the world, this is still true) that we were part of classic agricultural society. When you were born, "they" knew what you would do your whole life, and there was no room or desire for innovation. After all, that harvest has to get in, just like it did for the last twenty generations. Today we are harvesting things never dreamed of before (how many people really understand a mortgage-backed security—evidently not the people who were selling them), and so you need to be open to change.

Where to Do It?

You don't "seek" your inner monster. It is, after all, your inner monster—it's there already. Actually, your inner monster is probably in several subparts that pop up occasionally when you can't push them away.

> "Your work is to discover your world and then with all your heart give yourself to it."
>
> —Buddha

Sitting down in a room determined to reach your inner monster won't hurt. You are after all trying, and that is the key. But to find consciously what you have been hiding from yourself is hard, because you are so good at hiding it. You need to let the mind relax, become unfocused. How often have you struggled to understand something—the tension just making it harder, then you relax, and it is clear

Your inner monster will pop up when you least expect—you may be walking, shifting attention between tasks, and they pop into your mind. The monsters that you have been hiding from need to be let in, because they are you.

It is so hard to catch glimpses of what is pushed away. Especially when sometimes it looks like images from a funhouse mirror, distant and distorted. When things have been pushed away and rejected, they have to be coaxed in slowly, with acceptance of what they may look like.

You want a place that relaxes you. If quiet relaxes you, then find a quiet place. If music relaxes you, that is what you want. Some break from the maddening crowd, especially at first, is really important. After time, you will be able to call your monster in all circumstances and noise, but you need some quiet time at first. You want a darkened room, white noise if you are in the city, someplace you have some real control over.

You will be excavating buried dreams, hopes you have pushed away. Newly risen dreams have power, and finding them isn't pure pleasure. The dreams are angry they were pushed away, buried. The dreams don't completely trust you to bring them back. You don't need other distractions as you find yourself, which pull you away from finding yourself.

Visualizing Monsters

What does a monster look like? There is a scene in *Men in Black* where Will Smith is confronted with a street scene full of oozing and vicious-looking space monsters, as well as a cardboard cutout of a young girl walking down the street. He shoots the girl, because she was so out of place and thus she had to be the monster. Seems weird, but in the movie it was the right choice.

> "No one remains quite what he was when he recognizes himself."
>
> —Thomas Mann

Is there an image from a monster/horror movie that really gives you the creeps? Think about that image: what is it about the image that bothers you? Is there anything you like about the image and are rejecting?

Your rejection of monsters is what makes them fearful, not the monster itself. Your rejection of what you could become, and could change to be, has pushed them into the dark, where they loom. Don't be like the Jedi, spending their entire lives in fear of what they can't bring themselves to look at.

Different feelings can be their own visuals. What does "frustration" look like to you? What does "anxiety" look like? Putting a face on a feeling helps bring that feeling to you, make it more comfortable to work with. There isn't any reason why you can't have a number of visuals, dealing with various parts of you.

People traditionally have had a multiplicity of images that they keep within themselves for different problems and concerns. The Catholic Church has to issue stern edicts every so often, limiting the power of saints, for example, so that people don't start believing more in the saints than in the rest of the theological structure. Early in church history, there was a pruning of the angels and related hierarchy, because people were drifting toward lesser angels rather than focusing on the Trinity. Many religions view everything as spirit filled. In a way, we are going back to our nature as humans by finding our inner monsters. This is a conversation we could have had with the first wanderers out of Africa. Today we may have science, but underneath we are still the same hardwired creature.

As religions evolved, they commonly had a number of gods, who manifested different powers and aspects of human nature. Having those different gods allowed a person to focus on what seemed most critical to them at a given time. Many cultures still have the same polytheistic structure. To some extent, the gods, by showing different natures, made people more comfortable with their own selves.

Bacchus may have made people a little too comfortable with their feelings, but that is an individual choice. And then there are sprites, elves, and leprechauns—all the fantasy world creatures that really don't fit into the religious structure, but that people create for their own needs. Humans need these visuals, these different ways of thinking about the world and our self. Why else would they exist in all cultures at all stages in human history?

Finding your inner monster is another way of approaching yourself, but it is creating an internal definition, not buying a packaged product based on social definitions.

Finding your inner monster is seeking strength from what you are taught to fear. That is a big jump from running from our fears. Fears are strong. How much stronger would you be if the socially exiled part of you, your fears, were part of your focus?

The only way to understand your fears is to feel them. When they sweep through you, don't run, don't bolt, just feel them. You will be surprised at what they are actually; they take other forms to get your attention, but at their base, everything you feel is a cry for attention from a part of yourself you are ignoring.

Do you remember the little exercise to draw a picture of what you see as a monster? Did you do it? Do you still have the drawings? Try it again now and see if there is any difference. Is this a monster chasing you? Is this a monster that you like or one that you fear? Is this a monster you would like to have on your side? Is this monster chasing something?

There are lots of computer games that feature monsters of one type or another. There are lots of shoot-the-monster games, as well as games that have *you* play the role of the monster. In *World of Warcraft*, you can pick from all kinds of beings, some of which certainly act in socially monstrous ways. And in *Grand Theft Auto*, the whipping boy for the protect-society crowd, the monster is the hero, shooting, robbing, and selling drugs. The fact that this is how many in society actually live – before the game and now- despite all law and social mores against them doesn't seem to affect the attacks on the game.

There is a new game coming out called *Spore*. In that game, you can design life from a single-celled organism, which then evolves to a complex life system, like an Earth. It is a wonderful resource to generate monsters and play with new systems, if you want to try it. Soon enough it will be a reality for governments to create organisms, playing the same games for real.

Then there are the *Sim* games—*The Sims, SimCity*, and the various offshoots—in which you can create a society, grow a town, and make people act and respond as you want. Complete power, within the system limits.

Traditional social thought can't respond to these new ways of viewing and understanding. It isn't that the world has changed, but information about the world is more prevalent, and the systems get caught in lies and partial truths much more easily. Before, information was distributed to the masses came out when someone powerful had an ax to grind. Now information is everywhere, and comes out when anyone has an ax to grind.

You have to define and create the boxes you think in.

A man, about to die, calls his doctor, his minister, and his attorney to his side. He hands them each a third of his assets in cash and tells them to put the money in his casket after he dies. They dutifully promise to do so. A week later, after the man dies, the doctor, minister, and attorney are standing at the casket.

The doctor says, "I couldn't do it. I gave the money to medical research."

The minister says, "I couldn't do it. I gave the money for missionary work."

The attorney looks at them and disdainfully says, "I am horrified that you would so callously disregard the final wishes of a dying man. I will have you know that my check is in his pocket right now."

You have to expand the box- and watch your attorney carefully.

If you are scared and upset of something in a corner of your mind, then that is proof of how important it is to you. A strong feeling, exiled, just grows larger as it is ignored. You are losing both the potential strength of what you fear and the energy used in hiding it. You only have so much energy, and using energy to hide from yourself wastes time and yourself.

Bring that back into you; use the power of the feeling and the understanding of what you are avoiding to gain strength. Traditional approaches demand you overcome the vice, triumph over yourself by adopting a socially useful virtue. Drop all the overcome, triumph over language. Overcoming yourself? For what values and whose opinion? You become yourself, integrating and combining the parts, not throwing them out.

> "And if thine eye offend thee, pluck it out, and cast it from thee: it is better for thee to enter into life with one eye, rather than having two eyes to be cast into hell fire."
>
> —Matthew 18:9.

What kind of insanity is it to call on you to literally destroy yourself for their values? The people who preach are not plucking out their eyes. As we have seen, those values are designed to be impossible to live up to, so that you are under their social control. Casting the command in religious terms makes it almost impossible to respond to—all the better for the system.

Today's world has to look at the new. That ancient agrarian society dreaded the new because they lived on a knife's edge. Change that damaged the harvest meant people starved, and so change was absolutely out of the question. Better to have no eye than to see that dangerous "new." Today, we must have the new, because to stay in the system as it exists guarantees starvation down the road.

The hardest thing to realize about the new is that the way you look at things now can't bring the new, because you have already limited yourself to keeping the new out. Can you look back in your life, think about something new, and notice how you couldn't feel or imagine it until it happened (besides sex)? It is hard to do, because once you are familiar with the new, the magic feeling wears off, and you forget it ever was new.

Actually, thinking back about new things that worked is a good start, because by realizing how many new things did work, you start opening up several levels down. It's easy to just focus on the new things that didn't work, but that locks the system levels below consciousness.

Therefore, this is not a "rational" process. The brain research discussed earlier casts a certain amount of doubt on "rational" explanations. Just let go and imagine; it's the unexpected you are after. Reward yourself for trying. Not with that entire bag of chips, but with something small that you want. And don't try to change yourself at especially stressful moments. Deciding you will become something new when making a speech to five hundred people is not going to work well. Self-discovery is going to have its own stresses, and you don't need to carry old baggage into the process. We want positive, small steps and growth from within, not forced.

The next chapter has a fun section on visualization ideas for seeing your inner monster.

How to Do It?

Opening your mind to your monsters is opening your mind to the forbidden parts of yourself. Think about monsters in films, television, books, comic books, and graphic novels. Imagine you are that monster, if it has any interest for you. Don't try to get into monsters you are emotionally neutral to—you are after yourself, the monsters that reach you for whatever reason. The reasons a monster reaches you are not going to be obvious at first, because you are fishing in dark waters here. Don't push for "rational" reasons, don't force into a traditional logical structure. Understanding will come with time.

Don't force coherence: don't try to make things seem rational/logical to start. You are opening up to your actual self, opening to those thinking processes. Those are rational processes, but a different system than the official self uses. The actual self rational system, as it emerges, is going to be conflicting and different from the official self. Coherence will come with time and reflection.

Try to think outside what the creator of the monster intended. Don't limit your thought to the author's goals or imagination; think about whether the depiction makes sense in a system, or whether it was just randomly thrown in to advance the plot.

If that monster did exist, what would that monster want, what is it seeking, what would it be thinking? Flesh it out, think through what it would really do, not just some throwaway morality play points.

Visualize, don't articulate. This is active meditation, and your vision is you. Articulation is words, which you learn through social training—the words and the structure that the words fit into. Visualization, as your dreams show, doesn't have a lot to do with the social structure, but is really all you and your mind.

What do you feel? Feelings are inexact, and you have to be open. In the next chapter, we present the concept of the comfort zone. You want to relax your limits, so you need to be willing to let that internal thermostat spin a bit.

Try a monster in your mind-think about what a monster would feel in the system of that monster . What kind of system does a monster function in, the constraints, resources, opportunities? As you visualize different monsters, something will feel right to you, or something will feel wrong, which is telling you something about yourself. What do you feel warm about, as opposed to cold and uncomfortable? As we have probably beaten to death, what you are trained to feel as wrong is done so that you do as you are told, not because what you're doing is wrong per se, or wrong for you. Distinguish feeling tense/not socially acceptable from not connecting with the monster emotionally.

Once you have found something you feel comfortable with, you have taken a big step. Take those first few steps and visualize the monster surrounding you, emanating from you. When you catch yourself relaxing, breathing deeply and smiling, that is an image to remember and repeat. Go there , try this in difficult times. It's better than drinking or drugs, which are toys to dull yourself so you fit in. Real people make their own toys—they don't use off-the-shelf stuff.

Carefully notice the difference between modeling yourself on a character from a movie or book and reaching your inner monster. When you model yourself, you act, assess, and measure, evaluate against the character, and act again, which is a tense process. Reaching your inner monster is a relaxation of the body, not an assessment and measuring process.

Don't demand to know in words immediately what does it do for you; let it just grow slowly. Don't force it into words, because that imposes the structure of language on it. Let what you think gradually develop, and accept thinking different thoughts. In there, that is you, the exiled part.

Let your mind wander, kind of like early sleep—the parts of semi-consciousness where you start seeing pictures and stop thinking in words. At this moment, your mind, from several levels down, is talking to you.

Psychological Defense Mechanisms

If you are feeling as if you are fighting yourself, there is an enormous amount of information in the traditional psychological literature on the standard defense mechanisms against change. (Defense mechanisms actually occur in many situations, but we are focusing on focus on change.) Common compilations of those mechanisms include, among others, *denial, displacement, identification, isolation, projection, rationalization, reaction formation, regression, repression,* and *undoing.* An Internet search on any of these will produce lots of information, and you can also consult basic psychology texts from the library, so you don't have to spend any money if you are feeling averse to change and want help.

You have to be very careful about these labels. Labels are libels, and these terms are used for command and control, just like religious commands. Because these labels are "scientific," the medical community puts up the same resistance to their examination that religious leaders do. So don't just accept a label; look back at it. Like any social virtue/vice, if you just accept the label, you have already lost the discussion.

The essence of all of the mechanisms is ignoring reality. These are just different ways of doing that. Where you absolutely are ignoring reality it is going to always have bad ultimate consequences. Now, reality can be many different things to many different people, so there is that issue. And social realities, where accepted by the power structure, can stifle dissent by labeling the opposition with these terms. The concepts can be helpful if you step back and think about whether you are not dealing directly with something through one of these devices.

Denial is a refusal to accept external reality because it is too threatening. Sometimes denial is absolutely necessary: should you ever have to run at an enemy that is shooting at you, denying in your mind that you will die is very helpful. On the other hand, denying that you have to file your taxes is just going to make that external reality a lot more threatening in a short time.

Denial can be subtle and involve some of the other coping mechanisms at the same time. Studies show that we all constantly overestimate our abilities compared to those of others. Almost all of us consider ourselves better drivers than average, for example, which is statistically impossible. Confronted, we deny thinking we are better than we are, better than "them." It is a human trait to overestimate our abilities and underestimate the effect of random or uncontrollable events that affect us.

To put it another way, we all have a tendency to misperceive the causes of actions. We commit *attribution errors* (a psychological term) when we take credit for positive outcomes and attribute negative outcomes to external factors. Denying that we are the cause of negative outcomes, if we actually are, robs the experience of anything positive, because we learn nothing from it. Optimism is a good thing, except when we are fooling ourselves. Being optimistic (part of conforming to social reality) can produce some spectacular disasters. Better to watch from the sidelines than to be the explosion.

Distortion is a gross reshaping of external reality to meet internal needs. This book argues that society engages in this constantly, but that isn't what the psychological books generally mean. Ignoring reality, playing pretend about real things doesn't work at the individual level or the societal level.

Projection is attributing one's own unacknowledged feelings to others. So "you hate" turns into "they hate," for example. Taken to an extreme, this can be paranoia. Paranoia isn't good or fun, but remember the saying from the 1960s: Just because you are paranoid doesn't mean they are not out to get you.

Passive aggressive behavior is aggression towards other expressed indirectly or passively. For example, your children don't refuse to do things; they just don't do them. At work, the file gets lost, or the relevant information is always missing. Passive aggressive behavior is a lot smarter than active aggressive behavior, which elicits an immediate and negative social response. Still, dishonesty never works, especially when you are fooling yourself. You need to know why you are acting like that, because passive aggressive behavior almost always sparks an aggressive response eventually.

Acting out behavior is the direct expression of an unconscious wish or impulse to avoid being conscious of the emotion that accompanies it. This is a critical reason why the book advocates finding your monster, because these things happen. Acting out can be extremely damaging to the person, which is why you need to be in touch with yourself. Acting out by just following the motions of a poorly understood morality play is one of the most dangerous things you can do.

Intellectualization is the separation of emotion from ideas. It can be considered thinking about wishes in formal, bland terms and not acting on them. Intellectualization could be considered an extreme example of words fitting into a linguistic structure but really meaning nothing.

Repression is one of the favorite defenses. It is not noticing, including memory lapses and lack of awareness of you physical status. The emotion is conscious, but the idea driving the emotion is absent. Repression pushes down what is bothering you, so you don't have to think about it. But emotions don't push well, and they don't stay in their containers.

Reaction formation is behavior completely opposite to what one really wants or feels. The classic example is being a caregiver when you actually want someone to take care of you. Reaction formation is very dangerous, because it will work in the short term, but not in the long term. By the time your inner, actual self says NO, you will be well down the road and locked into something that you have been acting like you wanted very much. This is a problem that makes clear the difference between the official self, and the real self. The difficulty is that by the time it hits, the steps taken to support the official self make it far harder to find the real self.

Displacement involves separating emotion from the real object and redirecting it toward someone or something less offensive or threatening. This can be extremely rational, if, for example, what you are angry at is just too powerful to attack. But if you don't realize what you are doing, you will be dealing with a false problem that will never resolve itself. The classic social response is turning economic hardship into hatred of an ethnic or religious sub-group.

Dissociation is the temporary and drastic modification of one's personal identity or character to avoid emotional distress. This is a short term only fix. Like reaction formation, you can go a fair distance with this before it doesn't work anymore, which actually only makes things worse. Dissociation is a classic device in horror movies, where the packaged person steps aside and something else, unknown to all, steps out.

Sublimation is the transformation of negative emotions or instincts into positive actions, behaviors, or emotion. This can be a wonderful device for making the best of things. One has to be wary of rationalization, however, which is what this can very quickly become. Dr. Pangloss, in *Candide*, who always felt that this was the best of all possible worlds, is what you want to avoid.

The above just are one set of classifications and terms. There are many others, which define things slightly differently and weigh certain aspects more heavily. Thousands of books have been written on these concepts and their permutations.

Again, do treat the standard psychological texts cautiously. Their typical focus is increasing socialization, not rejecting it, and so don't take them at face value. But the concepts can be helpful in seeing whether you are fighting yourself or not looking at something directly. And beware of "medical student disease" when reading psychological literature, where every normal behavior suddenly acquires ominous (but expensively treatable) overtones.

All these concepts can be helpful in a clinical setting, where the behaviors at issues can be carefully determined. The problem that psychology faces is the essential lack of definition of many of these words. These words truly are like a pail of sand dumped on the ground. The central bulk is what most people hope they mean by the term, but there is a lot of room within that bulk, so it is very easy for people to use the same term and mean completely different things.

Then there are the grains spilling out away from the bulk, which other people may use for special concepts of theirs but not communicated the nuances of meaning to others. Finally, because of the impreciseness of the meanings, it is easy for people to make the words mean anything they want for the purposes they have in mind. The Soviet approach of institutionalizing dissenters for mental illness is a classic example. What makes matters more complex is that, within the Marxist dialectic and worldview, dissenters were clearly mentally ill. Outside the dialectic, focusing one's anger at a broken system crushing human rights seems rational. So who was crazy there?

Evaluation Ranges

If you want to take a rational approach, where would your monster rank on the following type of choices?

Would your monster prefer:

- high physical stimulation or low;

- does your monster have a daily structure (breakfast, pillage, lunch) or prefer to go with the flow;

- is your monster solitary, or does it hunt in a group like raptors do;

- does your monster rest/recharge it's energy alone, or at a monster bar/socially;

- is your monster's personality flexible (going with the flow), or does it have rigid guidelines it lives by (defining the flow);

- does your monster handle interruptions well, or eat anything that interrupts it (don't we all wish);

- and does your monster completely focus, or does it do multiple things at once?

Where do you rank now on those choices? What makes you comfortable or uncomfortable about where you are now? Why are you comfortable or uncomfortable—to impress others, to function socially, or what you sometimes quietly feel you would like.

In the movie *The Golden Compass* (and also in the book, which was much better), each person in the movie had a daemon, a linked and visible "spirit" in various shapes. As a person grew, his or her daemon changed, and froze when that person reached adulthood. One of the distasteful characters had his freeze into a scarab, which would tell people when you approached what you really were. If you play with that idea, don't limit your concept to the implications in that book, since the author had his own ax to grind. Play with the idea; make the idea and its growth your own. The book is copyrighted, but the ideas can be modified.

A daemon was considered to be an immaterial being, holding a middle place between men and deities in pagan mythology. All the pagan religions were (literally) demonized by the church, so you have to go back to the earlier concepts. As we have seen, control mechanisms are the lifeblood of society, and anything that can be brought into play for that task will be.

What in your life now would be considered unbelievably monstrous by the social groups you are in, if everyone knew everything? What would be different between the various groups you belong to? Why is that? What kind of a creature would do whatever it is, and in what context? What is actually being attacked by the monstrous acts? What do you think the other people in the groups are doing, or would do if they could?

Certainly, visualizing the negative figures can open eyes—perhaps make you glad it's not your monster, but that which is vehemently forbidden probably has some serious point behind it. As a political lesson only (skipping the religious issues) Lucifer's rejection of the Lord's authority and subsequent civil war is the most destructive event in a real world economy and society. You can see why that would be literally dammed.

When to Find Your Inner Monster? Surroundings?

In life, it is very easy to get wrapped up in preparing to do something rather than just doing it. It is common for university professors, in doing research, to become experts in computer techniques, which they did instead of the research that the computer techniques were supposed to be for.

Getting ready to do something is easy—you know what you are doing, you can fuss around and get a feeling that you're doing something positive. Deep down you know that cleaning the refrigerator instead of thinking about difficult things is avoiding the issues, but at least you will have food if you ever do start on the "doing." Part of this is a feedback issue: you are doing something that you get a response from, as opposed to doing something that doesn't seem rewarding, because it's hard to figure out what really happened. The *new* is like that, but you have to put aside the getting ready and *do* sometimes.

If you get really tense at times, just breathe—in through nose, out through mouth. Taking a few breaths calms a person down from almost anything. Tension and fear are biomechanical processes, part of the fight-or-flight response, and they involve a lack of oxygen to the brain.

It is so hard to drop your pre-conclusions and just look. The following quote by the famous detective Sherlock Holmes illustrates this:

> "You will not apply my precept," he said, shaking his head. "How often have I said to you that when you have eliminated the impossible, whatever remains, however improbable, must be the truth? We know that he did not come through the door, the window, or the chimney. We also know that he could not have been concealed in the room, as there is no concealment possible. When, then, did he come?"[26]

If you know what you want to do, you will find time to do it.

Opening to Understand the Dark

There are lots of monstrous things that everyone feels, by the traditional standards, because that's what the standards are designed to do. Knowing your monster and understanding where the conflicts are is certainly going to let you guide your life better than pretending to be someone you are not, having flashes of the real you pop up unexpectedly. Remember, disregard the traditional light/dark rules and roles as you think: this is exactly what you are trying to get away from. The good news is that this is a voyage of discovery, which is what life is all about.

What if you could be more focused, relaxed? How would you fill

---

[26] Sir Arthur Conan Doyle, *The Sign of the Four*, 111.

the time that you now spend fretting? Be careful that you don't fall back on bad habits as you start to see new things, because there is always a void when something old goes and something new is just beginning.

> "Some people die at twenty-five and aren't buried until seventy-five."
>
> —Benjamin Franklin

Because this is completely individual, seeking new ground, the excitement of discovery is completely yours. At different times, different places, you should expose yourself (no, not like that) to new concepts and ideas of monsters, not just those forbidden by your social constraints. Mentally embracing your inner monster, making that conscious step over the socially forbidden line, is a critical step to embracing yourself.

Chapter 16: Asking and Looking

"And I say unto you, Ask, and it shall be given you; seek, and ye shall find; knock, and it shall be opened unto you."

—Luke 11:9

"For every one that asketh receiveth; and he that seeketh findeth; and to him that knocketh it shall be opened."

—Luke 11:10

A more modern of the above might go as follows: "Ask and you shall receive. Seek and you shall find. Knock and the door shall be opened unto you."

Seeking, of course, means that we may find. Answered prayers deliver back to us what we asked for. That is why it is so important to know ourselves and know what we are asking for. Ask and seek for what you are told you should, and you may be unpleasantly surprised at what comes back. Ask and seek for what you are, and you may just strike gold.

We pretend that it is hard to follow our heart's dream. Actually, the doors are open all the time, and sometimes you have to struggle to keep them closed—like one of those comic episodes where the person is loudly calling for help for appearance's sake and frantically holding the door against the police trying to rush in.

Jung used the idea of synchronicity: there is an intermeshing of events, and suddenly you see what you are looking for. Perhaps it was there all the time, perhaps your looking created it, but there it is. The concept says that we change, and the universe expands and furthers change. Leap, and the net will be there- hopefully your leap will be so successful that you didn't need the net.

You are looking for yourself; you just have to ask and you will come out. Recognizing yourself as you come out is part of the fun. Now, you should not always expect that you are going to come out in a good mood. Very important parts of you have been roughly shoved in dark places for a long time, and they are probably surly. People around you, who have made plans expecting you to act for them in certain ways, are not going to always be happy when you discover yourself and that acting for them isn't yourself.

Don't get mad at what you find out; don't kill the messenger of your feelings, your vision, when it comes to you, because it is inconvenient or makes other things difficult.

To catch the ball, you have to want to catch the ball. We are all trained to think about what can go wrong—if we catch the ball, maybe we get tackled. It's a small step from there to setting up situations where you fail, because failure is known. Failure can be controlled, and people are there for support. Success? Maybe you make the touchdown, and if you are not used to winning, that's a new experience.

Comfort Zones

We are all fixed into a small range of the possible because it feels "good."

A comfort zone is an astonishingly powerful concept. We learn through our senses and we can visualize a comfort zone. Take the thermostat in your house: comfortable at seventy-five in the winters and seventy in the summer; turn it up to ninety, and it is uncomfortable, down to sixty, and it is uncomfortable again. Just like our house, we try and keep our emotional and mental systems at a comfortable level. However, the level that may have been comfortable in the past may not be as comfortable now, which is why we are feeling a vague sense of unease. Or the level may be comfortable to us but isn't meshing well with the outer world, causing more tangible unease.

It is really difficult to experiment with that comfort level. You have to do something new, to try something outside the range, and see where it works, and doesn't work. This is especially hard because the first few changes will probably have at least some negative consequences, as well as little support from your peer group. If your mind isn't fixed on the new, then the change is impossible.

How many times in your life did you try something that wasn't pleasant the first time, but was wonderful after practice? (besides chocolate or wine) That's the problem with the new—the rules you evaluate by don't work, because they can't see the pleasure in that new experience.

The actual dangers (keep the externalization to a minimum–let's keep on thought processes for a while) are far less than you think. We are pretty much ourselves, and we are going to revert to the DNA-driven metabolism that lies at our physical core. What is critical here is finding the real mean, where you are really comfortable at. What we are after is a comfort zone that you can develop from, not just be frozen in.

> "The most important thing is to not stop question-ing."
>
> —Albert Einstein

Your inner monster can take you outside your comfort zone. Don't like it? Go back. Start to see differently—try something again, experiment with a different perspective.

Make a movie in your head. You really always wanted to direct: acting was just part of learning the craft. Perform that segment of the movie according to the script, then redo it, changing the story-board and the script, seeing how it develops. The classic "jump" in a horror movie is the image of something breaking out of a person. Internalized, this fear of something different works to freeze you as you are, to restrict personal growth, your ability to see change in yourself. Practice jumps in your movie; practice seeing changes in you.

A recent article[27] on how to control your fears in a falling market is useful for dealing with any kind of fear. Dr. Kevin Ochsner uses the idea of "cognitive reappraisal." The experiment described in the *Wall Street Journal* was to look at pictures that would normally be shocking, with the mental choice of either (a) simply looking at the picture, or (b) reappraising the picture as you look.

Paraphrasing the article, if you just look without thinking, you respond naturally without trying to change feelings. Reappraising

---

[27]   Jason Zweig, The Intelligent Investor, Wall Street Journal, July 19, 2008

is actively reinterpreting the photograph, using your imagination to spin it into another, less emotional scenario that could have resulted in the same image. Emotions are malleable, but you have to realize that you can control your feelings. Part of the block to realizing how much control you have is that society doesn't really want you being able to step outside the lines. If you control your emotions in one area, then you might be able to control them in other areas they don't want you to go to.

So if you see a scary picture, it is possible to reappraise and re-interpret what is happening in a different way that isn't fearful. For example, they used a graphic picture of a wounded person, which is shocking unless you work in the ER. If you reinterpret the picture as from a horror movie, all makeup and plastic, the revulsion and reaction just vanishes.

Another method is to step outside yourself and imagine that this is happening to someone else. What questions would you ask that person about the situation, what would you need to know to give advice? Imagining it is happening to another. What advice would you give to that person?

The article concludes that you can, in any situation, control your cues. You can control what you choose to look at. Fear is contagious, so stay away from fearful people. Think, don't react. The amygdale, a fear center in the brain, can react in one twenty-fifth the time required to blink your eye. So don't let the brain see an attack where there is only a shadow.

Now, if you see a grizzly bear in full flight towards you, then let the fear reaction sweep through, and run like crazy. You don't have to be the fastest runner in the crowd, only the next to slowest. If there isn't a crowd, perhaps you should have given more thought to this situation before you stepped into it.

The fears in your mind are shadows. They are not the bear, but the mind can see them as the bear. So you react to your boss's criticism, the person who cut you off driving, and the spilled drink when you wanted to relax as if they were fight-or-flight events. As we discussed earlier, our behaviors are like a bag of sticks—we have only a limited number of choices, and it's too easy to use the wrong stick at the wrong time.

The harder your fears push, the closer you are to understanding them. They bolt, take new shapes, pull out old fears, and transfigure, just like the Terminator's ultimate enemy, taking whatever shape you jump at the most, like a boggert in Harry Potter. In Harry Potter, laughing at them makes them disappear, but we don't want to laugh at them. When we laugh, they will go away into the dark again and hide—and wait. We want their strength, their emotion, their power, and we want to understand where they are coming from.

When you find them, you may find that you have limitations. You may find that you can't do things you think you would like to be doing. Accept your limitations, if you are sure of them, and act accordingly—only a fool tries to spend his life proving to someone else what the other person thinks he is. Ignoring the philosophical issues of communication and understanding, this is a "good is them" trap—don't fall for it.

An article in the November 30, 2008, *New York Times*[28] discussed how to be calm. Dr. James J. Gross listed five methods in an example dealing with dealing with a difficult boss. The methods were,

- avoid the situation where possible (being careful not to run and carry the problem inside you);

- change your attention—focus on something other than what will upset you when talking to the person;

- cognitive change—define the situation mentally as you want, not as thrown at you;

- modify the situation where you can to reduce stress; and finally

- repression—pushing it down for a short time when necessary.

Those five techniques can be applied in any situation in which you need to calm yourself. You don't want a fake calm, but there are times to present that shallow social face until you are ready to show

---

[28] Kate Zernike, "Never Let Them See You Sweat", New York Times, November 29, 2008

yourself. Of course, this takes some practice. The hardest part, surprisingly, is wanting to be calm, wanting not to react. Thinking you should react, staying in that box where you have to react, is the most important step.

Monster Visualization

Physical Attributes

Open your mind: What would it be like to have a tail? What kind of tail do you see? What kind of tail do you want to see? What does one tail mean to you that another doesn't? Does your tail twitch like a cat's, does it wag like a dog's? Is your tail long and twisting, like a dragon's?

Dragons are almost a Jungian archetype, prevalent in almost all cultures. Huge, winged, with scales and teeth—all good monster attributes. Perhaps there is a racial memory of dinosaurs, burned into ancient mammals, who ran from the huge lizards. Do you see a tail long and skinny, or one that is hooked or forked at the end? What about monkey tails, prehensile tails that can grasp and hold? Have you ever thought that if the orangutans would have succeeded instead of us, they would have vines going to the upper floors of buildings instead of elevators? Imagine climbing with your espresso up a vine to your office.

Can you feel claws? Imagine how it would feel to be a cat, or a tiger, as those claws come in and out. You can look closely cats at as their claws go in and out—not many of us would care to be close to a tiger as its claws came out. Dragons have claws, but would your dragon have claws that retract or stay out all the time? What color would your claws be? What if they break—do they grow back? Are they steel or bone? What color polish would you paint them, if that's your monster? What do your claws do? What is your prey?

Wings—we all want wings. Ignore the physics issues—perhaps you are drawing on dark energy, and so the usual rules don't apply. Or maybe a little advanced engineering is involved, with really, really good batteries. Dragons have wings, angels have wings, and demons have wings. What would your wings look like? Long wings, short wings, heavy wings? Covered with feathers, leather, or perhaps a synthetic? Would they be like a tail, something to twitch, to spread and wrap around yourself? Would they be a weapon? A recent vampire movie had a vampire with sharp points at the ends of its wings, which were rather effective. It is effective power sources that really divide our world from science fiction movies—if we ever invented an extremely powerful, but light and portable power source, then wings, and lots of other things, would be simple.

Tongues and teeth—what does your monster have? And having those, what kind of a jaw and lips? You don't put six-inch teeth into a normal human jaw—for one thing, when you closed your mouth, you would spear your eye. It takes real bone to hold something like that, and that shapes the head and neck structure. Maybe you don't need huge teeth. Maybe you have metal teeth, or your monster likes salad. Is your tongue long and twisty, or is it stubby. What does your monster's tongue do?

Eyes are fun—you can pick your eye color, if you have always hated your eye color. And the shape: is the pupil round, or shaped like a cat's, or a different shape entirely as it sees a different light range? Do you want the usual red eyes of a monster, or maybe purple? What do your monster's eyes see—what spectrums, ranges—and where are the eyes located?

If you are going to have eyes, what about the bone structure or casing that the figure is in? Does your creature have brains like the Martians in *Mars Attacks* (hopefully your monster has a stronger resistance to country music than those monsters did)? Those are monsters that had a good time all the way through the movie, wiped out only at the end by the usual random plot device. Or is your monster from Jupiter, which would have either a truly massive bone structure or be very small as an adjustment to gravity?

Appearance

Do you want your inner monster to be physically gorgeous? Very attractive monsters have certain advantages, primarily that they can get closer to their prey before they bolt. What size do you visualize your monster? Larger than human, a *lot* larger than a human, or small, getting into interesting places you wish you could get into?

Maybe just leave it open, and the monster can shrink and grow as you wish.

Traditionally, the "good" figures have been gorgeous—angels, for example. As the good structures in society define the entities, they get to load for their side, and most people picking external shapes are going to go with the gorgeous. As men have traditionally defined many of the images, positive elderly male images have put growing older in a positive light so that competition against younger males for females can be won with tricks and treachery.

There is a lot to be said for the external that is huge and menacing. We are going for the internal here, so you can be anything you want, but don't be surprised at what you pick. Don't reject what you are visualizing because of appearance—something is being said to you; don't ignore it. And don't force what you pick. If you are female and pick a monster who looks like the Victoria's Secret women, they certainly may be monstrous in many ways, but forcing your monster to fit a socially defined role isn't going to work as well as you might hope.

Visualizing the external shape of your monster involves the organic. The "dark" is usually stuck with the negative organic images—sick, ugly, misshapen—all things that are politically incorrect. These are actually terrible judgment criteria. (How many gorgeous idiots are there out there?) The dark images were life images—of the Earth, beasts and creatures, from the water and out of the ground. There is no life high in the sky: life is down in the dirt, mud, and water.

Feel artistic? Want some visual feedback? There are many software programs you can model monsters in (Poser, ZBrush, 3DS, etc.) and games in which you can create a monster for yourself. You can just take a piece of paper and play with ideas—no points taken away for rough sketches. Children are happy to draw anything, until they are criticized for not reaching an "artistic" level. Pass on the artistic, play with your thoughts. Play with making monsters.

What sex is your monster—what sex *could* your monster be? What difference does it make? Monsters for men and women are probably quite different beings. Does a woman's inner monster have hairy legs and no makeup?

Calvin and Hobbes had a lot of cartoons about monsters. Talking about monsters under the bed, Calvin said, "They're all teeth and digestive tracts. No brains at all." What happened to those childhood monsters? Eventually, each of us becomes old enough to have a monster inside to handle those childhood monsters, even though we don't always acknowledge this to ourselves. If we didn't get to that stage, this is the time.

Imagine: when would you need that cold, expressionless face of a raptor—complete focus, no reserve? When would you need to act as a tiger—all action, all focus?

Abilities

What about resistance to the usual active social negotiation problems—bullets, swords, arrows? Can your monster take a punch, or a swing from a two-by-four? Society gives all monsters a weaknesses. Dragons, for example, may have a weak spot over their heart, because otherwise there would be no way to defeat them. Your inner monster is what you define. What would damage your monster, other than your neglect and repression? Certainly some things damage your monster, because there are things you care about, and defining those tells you all about yourself.

What abilities would you like to have? If you had them, how would they really change things? If you could move time and space, then so many things in normal life would become pointless, and would you have totally different concerns. Who cares about money if you can flit into a bank and grab some? A recent movie, *Jumpers*, was fatally weakened by lack of thought by the writer. If you can flit in and out of places, taking what you want, then you can flit in and out and neutralize the people trying to kill you who don't have your powers. The screenwriter showed a complete lack of ability to think outside the box.

Visualizing Feelings

How would you visualize various feelings you have? What does frustration look like to you? How about anger? Beyond the red eyes, what does your anger look like to you? Is envy the green-eyed monster to you, and why would it have green eyes? When you think about how society describes those monsters, doesn't it become more obvious how society defines you, your feelings, as a monster?

What about monsters that are nerve focused: anxiety, tension? Would they be hazy, indistinct? Would they spark with electricity? Would they have a structure like the outline of a person?

What would be a solid monster in your feelings? Touch is a real, physical feeling. Would that be a solid monster? What would touch, or the fear of being touched, look like?

And then the most difficult monster to visualize and reach: what does your official self look like to you? What kind of a monster does it feel like?

Thinking

What does your monster think like? Monster thinking in fiction tends to be pretty straightforward ("Hate humans") with an occasional heart-of-gold monster mixed in for political diversity points. Why would the monsters hate humans? Each of us can supply many reasons why we might, but why would the monsters?

Or maybe the monster doesn't hate humans, but it doesn't need them, at least in the way that humans do. In one of my favorite science fiction stories, "To Serve Man," aliens came to Earth and humans started believing they had come to satisfy their every need. In the last paragraph a human translates their guidebook (bearing the same title as the story) and discovers it is a cookbook. It was also a *Twilight Zone* episode. You have to like a monster with a sense of humor, who must have been chucking to themselves as they gave their speeches. It is doubtful that humans would really be all that edible—humans tend to be rather thin, as opposed to, say, buffalo. The recent shark attack in California where the shark left the person uneaten is an unflattering commentary on humans as food.

The real problem with cannibalism (a favorite movie monster) is that the bugs don't have a species barrier to jump, so cannibals get sick a lot. And don't get me started on the living dead: what possible system could be sustained by an occasional meal of brains? And if they don't sustain themselves on brains, what does keep them going-everything is subject to constraints. Unless, of course, they are powered by dark energy, which starts getting complex.

In a rather terrifying recent horror program, based on the short story "The Screwfly Solution," a virus was causing males to murder females. We picture the aliens like the ones in the *Independence Day* movie, all flourish and armed to the teeth. More clever monsters let the prey do the work for them.

Do you think that monsters would have the same fascination with human details that a human does? That's a shocking statement to humans—what could be more interesting than whether that person parts her hair in the middle or on the side, and what ancestry her nose shows? What would a monster be interested in, and what kind of things would it focus on? How would your monster think through problems in its dimension, and then how would that change how you think through problems?

Feeding and growing your monster is mentally gradually slipping into its skin. What you see the monster as, how you think the monster thinks, all leads to what kind of system the monster functions in. Thinking about the monster's system leads to thinking about the external systems thrown at you daily.

And if this seems too completely far out, the *Alien* movies showcased a creature that had to be bio-engineered. It was so vicious and destructive that it is difficult to imagine a world it could have evolved in, as it would have destroyed all food sources too quickly. It is like a plague that kills its victims too quickly to spread. In the first movie, the ship carrying the aliens was broadcasting a warning sign, and the pilots of that ship were not aliens—just alien food. As they had thousands of them on the ship, you can bet they were not carrying them as birthday presents. As a bio-engineered weapon to drop on your enemies, an alien from that movie would be about as vicious a weapon as could be devised. It won't be that long before we can bio-engineer all kinds of interesting things, and thinking about monsters is the best way to approach those possibilities.

Feeling and Seeking

If you open yourself, if you grow, how will you feel? Because you can't know the new, the new seems fearful and makes us want to stop thinking. It takes some time to come to terms with yourself, because the self doesn't always trust us. Why should it? We sold it out before, and we may again.

> "Not until we are lost do we begin to understand our-
> selves."
>
> —Henry David Thoreau

The official self is for control. Control is almost always a NO. No to this, no to that; this will go wrong—we become accustomed to all the accumulated no's that we hear over time. Doing nothing is almost always momentarily safe, although not enjoyable. At least with doing nothing, we didn't bring ambiguity into our life by making a choice we might regret. Of course, choosing not to do is a choice like any other, but not as obvious.

"If you're not a part of the solution, you're a part of the problem" was a famous quote from the 1960s, and it is just as true about your inner self. Doing nothing causes anger inside, which you will then vent at those that do something. Doing nothing causes frustration and depression, and (to be politically incorrect) that angry look that very large people seem to have. The look seems to say, "I know I don't meet social expectations," full of fury and suggesting they are dangerous to come near.

When exploring the new, you can pick pleasant things too. Scents that you like are a path to new associations and feelings. Sound can excite, relax, lull, stimulate, take you out of where you are, and ease the travel to somewhere new.

Scent is more important than we normally think. Play a game: buy a bag of high quality jelly beans. Sample them until you are comfortable with the distinctive differences between them. Don't buy another bag to extend the tests. Then sample the beans again with your nose pinched shut. Surprise, there isn't any difference between the beans. If you unplug your nose halfway, the scent returns, along with all the other memories and emotions tied to that scent.

We tend to ignore scents in the rush of life. They are not serious, we can't make any money off them, so unless we smell a gas leak, we tend not to focus on them. It is those kinds of ignored senses that one has to listen to. Hearing the same old social beat all the time gets numbing, and life is too short to be numb.

What if you could be focused, relaxed? All that inner noise abates—all that mental activity presenting a future, rehashing the past, you as hero and you as fool. Showing yourself as the hero, but with bad endings and admonitions to not do these things. What would you do with your time? How much of the regular daily mental process is just noise disguised and wrapped in a useful suit?

Touch is a wonderful tool for focus. If you touch something, you focus on that item, and the other noise drops away. Experiment with doing this deliberately. Allow yourself to be free of social anxiety.

When you find a view of yourself, a monster that you are comfortable with, then suddenly there is a quiet. There is almost a void, when the noise stops. It's an odd, and not entirely comfortable, feeling the first few times. Flip back and forth between various monsters, and feel the one that makes you relax.

Can you visualize the "noisemaker," the logical brain, as an entity? If you do, it probably isn't pretty, as its job is to say, "No, things are scary." When you visualize it, does it change? Does it get angry as it is touched? Can you accept that angry visual and not reject it? You want to that visual into the self, and use all that energy flowing out. The idea here is to eliminate all the battles you can, as the external world has more than enough challenges.

Chapter 17: Finding: Habit, Discovery, and Change

Driving a car takes about 5 percent of your actual attention after you have been driving for years. That's why people eat, talk on the phone, make notes, put on lipstick, and do all the other things they do to pass the time. Occasionally, driving takes 110 percent of your attention—that visual perception of slow-motion when the laws of physics take over is something that sticks with you.

Discovery and change are like that. Most of us put our lives on cruise control and let our attention wander to trivial but flashy things that grab our attention. Just like the cat that chases the laser pointer light on the carpet—even though it knows nothing is there when it touches the light, the cat will still stalk and attack it. So we spend our time focused on things that don't matter but are comfortable with.

When change comes, suddenly you are using more than the 5 percent that it takes to run on cruise control, because you are noticing a lot more things. Because it's change, you don't know whether what you are noticing is significant or not, because you don't know the feedback. Then when you add in the regular things in life, suddenly you are using 110 percent of your attention a lot of the time, which is very tiring after a while. That is why people relapse and quit, because it is easier.

Choices in life have to be made. You either select alternatives out of habit, or you choose a course of action.

If you validate all your opinions through other people, then this is going to be harder. If you are a chameleon, and all your opinions are the ones you absorbed from social situations, then this will be really hard.

> "If we do not change our direction, we are likely to end up where we are headed."
>
> —Proverb

Part of change is giving up old things. The reason you are changing is to give up the trivial, the things in your comfort zone, so let them go; don't carry them along. If you carry them along, you have confused filling time with doing things.

Visualize the process of discovery and change as pruning a wooded lot. You cut down and pull out the old, dying trees and weed out the scrub growth to let the new growth have space. It's tough at first, because suddenly the wind blows hard against the new growth, which had the scrub to block the wind. You notice the wind blowing and don't notice that now the scrub isn't stealing resources from you. You forget that the dead trees were rotting; you only remember that they were support. You have to expect that wind, and after some time, you will have grown and strengthened so that you no longer notice the wind except as a pleasant breeze.

Let's start by thinking about what to do tomorrow. Why not ask what to do today?

> "If one does not know to which port one is sailing, no wind is favorable."
>
> —Lucius Annaeus Seneca

What to do tomorrow: without your inner monster to help you look around corners and at the outside, you act out of habit. Habit isn't living; it is walking through the motions.

Why do people avoid change? There are lots of reasons. The logical part of the mind says we can't change, shouldn't change, and won't change. Most of us are reactive in life, and few of us are proactive. If you change then, well, then maybe:

People will be hurt.
People will be abandoned.
People will hate me.
People will be upset.

The whole "people think" calculation rapidity turns into a "I think this and they think that, but they know I think this, so that means I will do that, and they will think this knowing that I think that," *ad infinitum*. You can't know what someone else thinks: we are desperately trying to find out what *we* actually think.

The inner thought police also say things to discourage us:

I will be alone.
I will look like a fool, go crazy, die.
I'm too old/too sick.
I'm not good enough/don't deserve success.
Change won't work.

They are just words. They are really fearful words, and they are designed to freeze you, to stop you. The words are a belief about something that hasn't happened, that isn't even clearly expressed or defined. A hazy and unclear belief is not a truth.

No matter what you do, someone will hate you. Family and friends change themselves; why wouldn't they expect you to change? Your family knows you are crazy, and you know they are, so you don't have a lot to lose there.

You may not expect it, but people will like the new, changed you. That is the key part of every story we read—think about the Harry Potter stories. You have to let new people in so they can like you. All stories require that a person be open to new situations for the new and exciting things to happen.

All those "logical reasons" thrown out are enough to make a person just stop dead, which is really their only function. If you actually had a detailed plan, and in the plan there were some very significant downsides, then you should heed them. A simple "everyone will hate me" isn't anything at all except fear. What all those beliefs are shouting is that you are afraid. Core negative beliefs are scary, which is why they are trained in you. You are scared, and so you do nothing. Doing nothing, you become nothing.

There are several possible reasons why we seek change. Actually, changing yourself is very difficult. Think about your handwriting: it probably looks much the same at fifty as it did at twenty, as it is a biomechanical process run several levels below consciousness. What this book is after is discovery of the real self, of your possibilities. We are not after you to change into something someone else values: this book wants you as fully you.

So "change" in this chapter is a little different from the usual definition. Change is the discovery of you, and moving to that you. As part of discovery, you will want to change certain behaviors tied to the past. Changing the rewards for behaviors will change those behaviors, which is a very significant improvement in your life. The "you" is pretty fixed—a comforting thought if you feel lost. After all, everywhere I go, there I am.

Change can be,

Proactive: Change that comes when we seek the new.

Reactive: Change that comes when we have no choice. Our present actions can't be continued, typically because of some external, real-world changes.

Due to fear: Change that comes when we are running from something. With this kind of change, one problem is, how can we be open to the new when we stumble across it? How can we avoid being so focused that we run right by opportunity?

Part of the problem with change is that it affects people we know. People have their own battles, and they may not want us to change. People put themselves in little boxes for safety, even though they may be unhappy there. If you open your box it shakes theirs, so their fear of change is pushed on you.

We would like to think that change to seek the new is what we do, noble and brave. Sometimes we do, but change because we have no choice and change because of fear is what happens most of the time. There we are, fat, dumb and happy, and we hit a wall or something comes out of the side that we were not expecting, or maybe hoping not to find.

Change because we are seeking the new is better, because you have more time. Through research and review, you can generate a list of options, which are in short supply when you have to react immediately to a new situation. To paraphrase Benjamin Franklin, in times of difficulty, you can trust money in bank, an old wife, and an old dog.

People will react to the same situation differently, depending on whether it is presented in terms of gain or loss. Your strongest emotional motivation is the probability of loss. Seeking change for gain gives you the option to stop and go back to the status quo. Seeking change to avoid loss means you can't go back to the status quo: you have, to some extent, burned your bridges. Frame your actions in your mind so you see a loss if you don't find your inner monster, and your motivation will be much stronger.

For all the talk about change and revolution when I was younger, the formal social structure is very resistant to change. Castro in Cuba is a clear example. His socialist paradise turned into a frozen social structure based on twisted views of Marxist/Leninist, whose primary purpose was to keep Castro and his associates in power. Look at the structure now: it is still the same people that fought with him in the late 1950s. That is consistent with other "revolutions"—the initial group around Lenin stayed in power until they just died of old age or incorrect political thought, as they did in China, Vietnam, and other counties which had a "revolution."

The unfortunate joke about the Russian revolution is that the most hated people—the Okhrana, the czar's secret police—often found good jobs in the Cheka, the Soviet secret police, once the revolution had settled into a structure. Things really didn't change, just the preferred social verbiage, and experienced secret police always have a place.

> "One of my favorite philosophical tenets is that people will agree with you only if they already agree with you. You do not change people's minds."
>
> —Frank Zappa

In reality, there are few points in personal life where real change occurs. Obviously as a child, one's body is changing until the late teens, but that happens in a pretty fixed structure: school and home. After school, there is work. A well known book on life planning, *The Three Boxes of Life*, focuses on school, work, and retirement, trying to mix them up, break open the box limits, and see possibilities.

Much if not all of advertising is merely an attempt to make you believe that a major positive change in yourself will come from changing the soda or beer you drink or the car you drive. We all know that there really isn't much change there, but it is an easy choice.

If you are not going to act out of habit, then you are looking at "change." Niccolo Machiavelli expressed the problem of change:

> It must be remembered that there is nothing more difficult to plan, more doubtful of success, nor more dangerous to manage, than the creation of a new system. For the initiator has the enmity of all who would profit by the preservation of the old institutions and merely lukewarm defenders in those who would gain by the new ones.[29]

That quote is at least as applicable to internal change as it is external change. Social, external change is even easier, to tell the truth, because that is someone else changing, our social face. Internal change is real change. Redefining our rewards for our actions—that is really hard. The *new* is unknown, like the edge of the medieval maps. Let's ask what to do tomorrow, rather than today, because we are thinking first.

> "By three methods we may learn wisdom: First, by reflection, which is noblest; Second, by imitation, which is easiest; and Third by experience, which is the bitterest."
>
> —Confucius

What do we do tomorrow? That terrible question that habit defines and social tradition freezes. How often to you really ask yourself

---

[29] Niccolo Machiavelli, *The Prince*, (Modern Library College Editions, 1950) 21

what to do tomorrow? Asking that after you lose your job (and your significant other takes the furniture) is a little late, although it does add some focus to the question. Asking how to pay the credit cards when the balance is $65,000 is probably the wrong question, as payment probably isn't possible then.

> "We have run out of money, so we are going to have to think."
>
> —Ernest Rutherford

That quote would be funny if it didn't happen so often. Throwing money at a problem is the easy thing to do, until the money runs out. People don't plan to fail; they fail to plan. What this book is arguing that even when you do plan, if you don't know what you really want, your plan isn't a real plan.

Why not ask the question before crisis is here, sitting and smiling in your living room like your cousin three times removed, who doesn't bath very often? Ask while there is still time to adjust and avoid.

If you want certainty, well, there is eventually death, the government will want more of your money than you want to give them, and you will be hungry five hours after eating. But real certainty is the necessity to make the decision: What do I do tomorrow?

The easy decision, and the typical one, is to do what you did yesterday. But when you do the same thing, is this a decision you made, or are you simply reacting to others? Are your actions the result of a series of compromises that have taken your life plans outside your original parameters?

> "Before you can break out of prison, you must first realize you're locked up."
>
> —Author Unknown

Life expands into all possible segments that it can fit into. Humans expanded from the relatively lush parts of the world into the fringes, in astonishing ways. But fitting into the fringes can create blinders that make change very hard to adapt to.

For example, why would anyone, if they had a chance to chose, be an Eskimo (Yupik/Inuit)? You freeze, you starve, and in the past had to expose your children on the ice, because taking on too many mouths could destroy the whole tribe. You allegedly had more words for snow than anyone else (although that seems to be questioned now), and you are proof of the ingenuity of the human species in facing adversity. There is no doubt that the utilization of extremely limited resources in very clever ways, and the adaptability of the human body, was amazing. Of course, the people who appreciate your ability tend to stay in warm climates themselves.

If you don't know about California, and you think that the snow and cold is all that there is, then you don't have any choices. More seal blubber tonight, please. That's why you need to see around corners and discover bright, warm places. After you discover those places, or find that you knew about them but are repressing the knowledge because they cause too much conflict, then you can make choices. Maybe you just really like whale blubber and being chased by polar bears.

The problem that the Eskimo's seem to face now is that with modern technology, much of the clever devices they traditionally used have been abandoned. With an identity tied to traditional behavior that no longer functions, the group is adrift. When adopting the new is a rejection of the group, and adoption of the old is futile, you get a lot of individually destructive behavior.

That doesn't apply just to Eskimo's, or to any other traditional group that has been marginalized. It is each and every one of us, tied to taught and traditional behaviors that just don't work well going forward.

We all look at other people and wonder why they do what they do. Is it clear that those are bad ideas? We don't ask ourselves the same question about tomorrow: we are Eskimos' and proud of it. And the author's know that they will hear from Eskimo's who are proud of their native traditions and history. Again, their struggle for survival against enormous odds is amazing and impressive. But if you were rationally choosing, not just going with what is presented to you, would you rather take California than a life north of the Arctic Circle? Doesn't some thought need to go into this?

Did you ever wonder why Charlie Brown continually made the same mistakes over and over? Why would anyone stay friends with Lucy—vain, arrogant, continually tricking Charlie Brown by pulling away the football? (Fool me once, shame on you, fool me twice, shame on me–Did your parents tell you this over and over? I think an interesting book would be a compilation of annoying but righteous parental sayings) And Lucy was shown as a therapist. That's putting a wolf to guard the sheep. Good Grief! Why didn't Charlie brown ditch that shirt, move to the city, and get a life? But how many things that we think and do each day are internalized from cartoon strips, which sink further inside us without thought? Those characters do the same things over and over, so maybe it isn't so bad for us.

Besides human nature being slow to change, of course the system doesn't want change. Things are difficult enough for the leadership as it is (deciding on rich food and fine wines) without having to worry about people doing what they want to do.

The *Inner Game of Tennis* book had an excellent suggestion: children don't unlearn a bad habit; they start a new habit. They don't unlearn crawling; they learn walking. So start new habits, and don't define them as fighting an old habit.

Dopamine Receptors and Choice

Many of the most critical decisions in your life are made by the dopamine receptors in your system. For better or worse, you do what your brain chemistry rewards. A therapist friend of mine, who has spent his life working with addictions of one type or another, said that when a patient walks in and says, "I never felt normal until I did _____" (insert liquor, crack, cocaine, heroin, etc.), then your job as therapist has hit a wall. The brain will keep doing what it likes, regardless of the consequences. In that case, you have lost an important life lottery if your chemistry loves those things. All of us have addictions; the key to a successful life is that the addiction has more upside than downside.

The conceptual split between physical health and mental health has been gradually ending, as it is clear that brain chemistry, although much harder to see than a broken arm, isn't any less real or physical.

The focus on "willpower" has turned out to be a dead end for most addictions: the eventual success, even from twelve-step programs, is so low that much may simply be due to brain chemistry changes in certain individuals as they age. The real losers don't experience chemistry changes, and society brands them as weak and low to make itself comfortable about walking away from that problem.

While it is easy to point to an individual and condemn the awful, but frankly limited, damage that their acts cause, the question not asked is, what damage are government and institutional systems doing and justifying with good reasons? You have to draw a larger box to see all the sides. The criminalization of recreational drugs in the United States, which has grown into a huge self-perpetuating enforcement system, certainly comes to mind. Dwight Eisenhower warned about the military industrial complex, but no one seems worried about the righteous alliance of the PPP (the police, prosecutors, and prisons), which only budget limitations can restrain.

The bright side, if you are worried about invoking your inner monster, is that, for better or worse, there are real limits on how far one can go with monstrous thoughts. Your dopamine receptors are pretty much hardwired. You are not going to redo your hardwiring by thinking any more than you can shrink your nose by picturing it really, really hard: what you will discover is your real wiring.

So what do you do tomorrow? How do you pick a course when predicting the future is so difficult?

You can only act on what you see as right and adjust for change. So your feeling of what you should be working on is what you need to cherish. If you are working on a pile of Oreo cookies instead of that project you tell people you are working on, trash the project, because you are not going to do it. I love Oreo cookies too, but you can only numb yourself so long with them to avoid doing something you don't want to do. The project you avoid can tell you a lot—why are you avoiding it? Why do you hate it? Learn that from it, not that you are a failure for not doing it.

You Really Can't Plan the New

How often do we see a biography where the best work was accidental, or started for totally different reasons than the end result

165

produced? Actually, when do you *not* see a biography where almost everything was accidental, if truth was told? People often blur over the plan and focus on the results, because it looks better if it seems you accomplished your goals. Moving the goal posts has a long and honored history.

Looking at things from a different perspective, given the rush of life—eating, sleeping, traveling, and social interaction—it's amazing that anything gets done at all. Have you ever filled out a daily diary listing what you did at all times? They are not fun, because it is astonishing how much fluff fills the day.

David Allen, in his excellent book *Getting Things Done*, says that there are three types of work: (a) Doing predefined work, (b) Doing works as it shows up, and (c) Defining your work.[30]"

The first two consume most of our time, personal as well as work. It is the third, defining your work/life, that we are focusing on here. It's hard thinking.

People in trading environments—financial traders, merchants, money changers, all the people generally condemned by traditional religious systems—have to face the what-to-do-tomorrow question every moment. Part of the reason those professions are condemned is that their questioning sometimes comes home from work, and asks powerful people the questions that they don't want to hear. They confront the "do tomorrow" decision and have to act. It isn't easy: if you manage money, and have to (no choice) invest $100,000,000 tomorrow so that it goes up (not down), you don't get to waffle on that decision. No wonder they retire early. The key thing that they learn is that they may not be right, and they factor that into the decisions.

The recurring financial debacles just illustrate that they don't make those decisions any better than anyone else. When you invest, remember: when someone says "it's different this time," run away (or sell short). Too much of the wise commentary in the mass media is the equivalent of running in front of a steamroller picking up dollars. It works for a while, but eventually you trip.

The clearest way to make a bad choice about what do to tomorrow is to assume, without thought or alternatives, that life will

---

[30] David Allen, *Getting Things Done*,(Penguin Group, 2001) 196

be as it was. The choices of the Jews in Germany before World War II comes to mind, but most of the Jews had actually left Germany. It was pretty clear that a train wreck was coming. The Jews in the neighboring territories were the luckless ones. Many had assumed (or hoped) that the problems would stay in another country, and they then had to confront a hugely changing situation and make some life-changing decisions very quickly. Many didn't, or couldn't, and paid a terrible price for assuming tomorrow would be the same as yesterday.

The same price was paid by the bourgeoisie after the Russian revolution, even though many of them didn't really think they were bourgeoisie. The same again in the Great Proletarian Cultural Revolution in China. In all these cases, a significant part of the surprise was how quickly their social structure turned on them: fear, avarice, hidden hate, social conformity, and combinations of the preceding.

Therefore, you have to ask yourself if your tomorrow is being dictated by others, narrowed by possibilities you are not considering. If you string your tomorrows together, then that is your life. As John Lennon, said, "Life is what happens while you are busy making other plans."

> "Never look back unless you are planning to go that way."
>
> —Henry David Thoreau

As we probably beat to death earlier, you don't want to (and actually can't) change yourself, what you do need is to know yourself. What the book keeps repeating (repetition can be effective; you can't dance without a beat) is that people don't make changes because they don't know what want, but because they are not in touch with the self. If you are not in touch with yourself, and the river of emotion isn't flowing, then there is going to be a lot of resistance to change.

> "You can outdistance that which is running after you, but not what is running inside you."
>
> —Proverb

A traditional way of asking questions is using a Strengths, Weaknesses, Threats, and Opportunities analysis. It doesn't have to be all encompassing or a formal project—these tend to be better "back of a napkin" plans, elaborated on over time as ideas come. The real problem with the rational analysis, shown in the chart, is that it hasn't let in all the choices. The rational, by definition, is a set of rules tied to given values, and so has the outside of the boxes clearly defined.

But not listening to the inside won't work. Everyone sits down with a piece of paper and produces something that the official self thinks is okay. But no one acts on it, because there is an emotional disconnect there. The rational analysis has ignored most of the real potential feedback to reach a predetermined selection. Try doing this as you open up to your inner monster, and you will see the entries change a lot as things open up.

As you think about change, remember the sled dog joke: if you are not the lead dog, the view never changes.

Habit means not thinking. The most destructive thing in life is un-thought compromise. If you get nothing else out of this chapter, the following is critical to your life.

Compromise and the River

Compromise is how life goes wrong. Visually, a river flows from high ground to low ground, cutting the channel through the soft soil, finding the path of least resistance to the water pressure. And there is pressure: more water is coming every moment, and it has to go somewhere.

You start with a life plan. Implicit in that plan are the parameters—the boundaries outside which the plan just doesn't make sense anymore. If you are driving somewhere, you stay on the road because cars don't do well in swamps—it's the nature of cars.

Time goes by. Ten years later, just like the river, you are way outside the boundaries that you set up. The car is in the mud up to the fenders. If you are feeling frustrated, strained, pulled—you are trying to be Dr. Reed Richards, the rubber band man, holding together the ship.

A classic analogy in the MBA program was the boiled frog (don't test this). If you put a frog into a pot of cool water, the frog is happy. If you rapidly raise the water temperature, the frog will jump out. But if you very slowly raise the water temperature, the frog's sensors never hit a "jump" point. Eventually, you end up with a boiled frog. You don't want to be a boiled frog, and that means you have to watch for slow cumulative changes: the river slowly moving its banks.

One of the most critical problems with this type of change is that when you are outside parameters, people ignore/misread feedback because the feedback is disturbing. Then nothing is done until things are hopeless, at which time people complain about their bad luck.

When you think about the future, do you go through alternative choices? When you go through the alternative choices, do you pretend that what you are doing now—the status quo —is analyzed the same as any other choice? Everyone does it, even large corporations with formal planning staffs: they carefully look at the risks and rewards of new choices, but not examine the status quo.

In a very formal analysis, a person sets a goal: be worth $2,000,000 in X years. Then he reverse engineers the goal: what has to happen in the intervening years to reach that point? There are many possibilities, and one tries to come up with possible and actionable plans. What people don't do is apply the same analysis to what they are doing now, seeing what that would lead to.

After all, we are getting by now, so the status quo must be working. The implicit assumption that doing nothing different has a low risk is a seriously flawed assumption. You need to treat the choice of doing nothing, just continuing on, as rigorously as any other choice. After all, if you are dissatisfied with something and considering changing, then there is something in the status quo that is bothering you. Not analyzing the status quo misses that something, that nagging feeling, and just pushes it aside.

> "Four things come not back. The spoken word, the sped arrow, the past life and the neglected opportunity."
>
> —Arabian proverb

An article in the *New York Times* said that location tracking data from cell phones in Europe showed that people frequent only a few areas and don't travel very far.

Duh, as if we didn't know that. But it makes us confront how little time in the daily routine we have for change. By the time you sleep, eat, work, shop, and consult the bathroom, your true discretionary time very limited (and if you watch TV, there went the rest of it).

"Everything flows; nothing remains."

—Heraclitus

So thinking about tomorrow is hard, because it's difficult to see outside the boxes we set or are given. Your inner monsters bring out the emotional, the feelings, the visualization, the outside to break through those boxes—as well as the strength to face the fears that stop us looking outside the box. So we move to action:

"In the long run, men hit only what they aim at. Therefore, though they should fail immediately, they had better aim at something high."

—Henry David Thoreau.

Remember the comfort zone discussion? Change is resisted because the transaction can be various shades of unpleasant. Especially if we were caught in a reaction formation, and hit the end of what the official self could force us to do, changing to our real self is going to be painful, with a healthy dose of social embarrassment thrown in.

When we resist what our inner monster might show (or where it might take us), we often experience a shaking, out-of-control feeling. We want to slam down the flow and regain our sense of control; we want to slam on the psychic brakes. We all have different types of brakes, numbing tools. Some are food, alcohol, work. Think about what makes you angry to even think about giving it up, even though you may know it isn't good for you. That is your key brake. While we all know that cars don't work well with the accelerator and the brake pushed at the same time, we run our own lives like that, wearing everything out.

Water at standstill is stagnant. All that pond scum forming, and a bad smell. You always know when you choose against your greater good, but it is easy to do. It is hard to walk away from blocking devices. The devices work, and even if you are not happy or comfortable, at least you have been here before.

Workaholism is a process addiction, which is an addition to a behavior. Substance addiction is obviously addiction to substances: food, drugs, alcohol. Additions are part of us, and, if positive, can be a wonderful thing. The happiest people are those focused on and doing what they most care about. But addiction to a numbing device will not bring success or happiness, no matter how much money or social approval it brings in. Behavior addictions are harder to catch, especially where they are socially accepted behaviors. Japan actually has a word for death by overwork (*karoushi*), which isn't surprising, because of the high degree of socialization in their system.

Blocking, freezing the official self, is to fear where we are going. If we stop ourselves from going, we give in and feed the fear.

CHAPTER 18: FEEDING AND GROWING YOUR MONSTER

"The opportunity to secure ourselves against defeat lies in our own hands, but the opportunity of defeating the enemy is provided by the enemy himself."

"Opportunities multiply as they are seized."

—Sun Tzu

You Don't "Use" a Monster

First, and this may seem contrary to what we have said before: You don't use a monster. Monsters don't manipulate.

If you want to use your monster within the boxes you think in now: for example, mentally having it crush what annoys you the most—it can be an emotionally helpful interlude. But "using" a monster means that you are imposing another set of values outside of the monster. You are not really looking at thing differently; you are just operating in the same system, with a bigger club, as it were, to whack the same buttons. In that case, are you covering up what the monster can bring to your vision?

Granted, pretending to use a monster is good, because you are playing with the ideas. We have to play with ideas before letting them be part of us.

Systems Thinking

A pivotal moment in my MBA program was when a professor asked the class what kind of financial results would occur from a given action. Looking disgusted at the blank stares, he said that you just start with a small part of the model and work it back up through the system—you reverse engineer it. With thought, research, and (a lot of) time, you could reverse model GM from the scene you see at the car dealer. How did the car get there, what kind of margins must the dealer have, so given necessary margins, what is the required cost, what are direct and indirect costs allocated to what, and away you go. It demands thought, which is painful, but it is really astounding what can be essentially reverse engineered from a particle of the product. Reverse engineering is backing into and understanding a system.

That was probably the most useful idea I learned from my MBA program, so you can skip two years of your life and a considerable sum of money. Whether you want to keep the drinking on weekends that seemed to be people's favorite part of the program is really your choice.

I have to warn you that system thinking can lead to dissatisfaction with the world. Pointless television plots, cobbled together from flash cards with no underlying system, do seem less enjoyable. Sound bites from politicians are more clearly seen as almost random utterances, wrapped around generalized social markers that can't be attacked. If you get bored, write your own speeches or television programs. Your work will be better than what is on the screen.

I often wonder how common it is for the endings of TV programs, movies, and other packaged entertainment to be dictated at least partially by the probation requirements of the various directors and producers. Hopefully that can explain some of the really random and pointless plot twists and lurches that we see.

The same reverse engineering approach works on any system, not just financial processes. Therefore, from a small part of a monster, you can work backward into that monster's system and explore new worlds and ideas.

Habits: How and Why

The major consumers products companies, such as Colgate-Palmolive and Procter and Gamble, have spent years finding out how to change people's habits. It is critical for them to establish a new routine for millions of people, so they can sell whatever pops out of the lab.

As they discovered, you can only go so far in selling to existing habits. An existing habit is a competitive market, which generally has existed for a while, and certain brands have dominant positions. But if you can start new habits, then you are the brand and you control that segment.

The key to habit is to tie defined behaviors to habitual cues in each person's environment. As much as 45 percent of what we do every day is habitual. Habit is doing something without thinking in the same location or time, usually based on cues in the environment. All you need is a subtle cue to jog the memory and kick off linked behaviors.

Paraphrasing an article from the *New York Times*[31]: there are four types of general cues. The critical cues are (1) a specific location, (2) a specific time, (3) a set of actions/emotions, and (4) specific people. Really, what else in life is there to tie a response to? If you tie an action to a specific cue, you discover that you lose the ability to choose your actions after a while. If you eat chips while watching football, you are going to just eat those chips even if you are not hungry. And don't start midnight snacks, as the stomach doesn't forget the new routine!

So if you are going to form a habit, you have to find a regular cue to tie the sequence of actions to. Likewise, if you want to break a habit, you need to figure out what the starting cue for that set of actions is and avoid that cue.

This is why beer commercials no longer feature young, busty, partially dressed women in their ads. The ads now feature groups of guys. So when a group of guys get together, out comes the beer. The problem with the young, busty partially dressed women is that (1) their actual physical presence is a fairly rare cue in real life, and (2) in those rare cases that the young women are present, other things pop to mind besides getting a beer. But a group of guys getting together, to watch a game for example, is a constant.

This habit formation pattern was used in a public health campaign in Ghana to persuade people to wash their hands after using the toilet. The ads didn't even focus on hand washing; they focused on contamination from the toilet, by showing the people with purple hands leaving the toilet, ruining everything they touched. Once people were disgusted by the idea of stuff on their hands, even if they couldn't see, smell, or feel anything on their hands, they started washing their hands.

---

[31] Charles Duhigg, "Warning: Habits May be Good for You", *The New York Times*, July 13, 2008,

So if you want to work on feeding and growing your monster, you need to create a habit. The habit can be your thinking, it can be your writing, or it can be opening your mind. All you need to do is to follow the rules: define a cue (again, a specific location/time of day, a certain series of actions, particular moods, or the company of certain people). Finding your monster doesn't seem like a group activity, although you may want to develop a way of going inside mentally to escape the presence of certain people. If you are in Dilbert's world, and can mentally withdraw from the cubicle pandemonium, there are many advantages to that.

Rewards for Trying

The key to feeding and growing your monster, as with any behavior change, is to reward yourself on a regular basis. Be kind to yourself in small, concrete ways. Never yell. Let your anger be a driver to reach what you are trying to grow to; don't use your anger against yourself.

Positive reinforcement is the key to behavior change. Small, regular rewards are the best, because the attention span waivers. Promising yourself that after three years of work you will buy the condo in Vail is pretty poor motivation, because it's too big and too far away. A candy bar on a regular basis (fine, fruit) is far better, and the best is to define certain actions that get immediate rewards after completion. Don't cheat yourself—don't skip a reward, because the unconscious (and monsters) don't forget.

Negative reinforcement (pain) isn't as effective as you might think. Depending on the action, negatives—pain, humiliation, etc.— can just be part of the ultimate high. How can that be? Think about heroin addiction, cocaine abuse, and really heavy drinking. When people do them, they know it's going to hurt, but that is part of the pop. They charge along, losing respect and friends, and none of that matters—it actually becomes part of the high, perhaps by starting from a lower place. Medieval monks wore hair shirts for penance to punish themselves for their greater glory, so being angry at yourself for failing can just lead to enjoying being angry at yourself.

People can make a virtue out of deprivation, which works for society by minimizing the goods needed. Then people use less, which is good, and they are focused on what they are missing, which keeps them from looking at larger issues. Don't do that.

Simply setting a small goal and accomplishing it is more of a reward than we realize. That positive feeling of accomplishment, of hitting the target, is a bright spot in the day. To judge an action, you need feedback, a response to evaluate by, and people will do useless things that reward them. Hijack that system, and do something useful that you get a reward for.

A little authentic luxury can go a long way. What constitutes pampering to you? What is something (the small things are the best) that is really pleasant and something you don't let yourself have often? Give yourself those things when you try something new.

Thought is nice, but you have to act. Doing something—writing, planning, some concrete physical action—is a necessary step. Growth/discovery requires action. You are responsible for yourself, and you have to do something to feel better. It is easier simply to stew about things, to think about how they should be different, how it isn't fair. Much of what we think about every day is just obsession about nothing to keep us from having to take action. Fretting about what movie star did what new stupid thing keeps us from having to attend to ourselves.

It is easy and socially encouraged, to have an active addition to anxiety. Society is happy with low-grade pain and an occasional panic attack, because you are just churning and have to turn to allowed rituals to get by. It is much harder to do the daily drudgery of small and simple daily steps to a goal, especially when the goal is the *new* and possible conflict with other people.

Be careful how you describe your behavior to yourself. There are a lot of negative names that are not always correct. For example, laziness is an important social code word. If you are lazy, then the fault is within you. Not the project, not the plan, you. Instead of lazy, are you really afraid of failure, of success, of abandonment, of not being good enough, or of not finishing? There isn't anything to be ashamed of in being afraid of those things: everyone is at times. But you can't let them stop you. Or are you really doubting the project and the plan, and so not acting?

Enthusiasm is fun. When was the last time you were really

enthusiastic about something? What got you out of bed fast and you went right to it? Enthusiasm is grounded in play, something that isn't graded or evaluated. Children don't have to be encouraged to play; they run to it. We, as adults, would be in much better shape, emotionally and physically, if we would skip excitedly down the sidewalk more often. Maybe do it when no one is watching.

Success is built on failure. Remember the moving goal posts: it is so hard to succeed at something that the world moves the markers to win. Don't fool yourself by moving the poles too easily, but keep in mind that the original goal isn't always set in stone. Don't over-imagine the problems to come, because solutions will appear at the necessary time for those problems.

Lack of money isn't a real issue. If your goal is to travel the *Queen Elizabeth II* around the world, and you don't have a dollar, then get a job on the boat and cook. You can wander around when off duty. Lack of money is an easy stopping point, and it should actually be phrased, "I don't have enough money to do this (and all the other things also)." The only real limit is lack of time.

As you change habits, make sure that you practice self care. At regular times, make a habit of that. Make sure that you give yourself the luxury of time: if you are too busy to enjoy pastimes, then what are you doing? What gives you true joy? What is true luxury to you? Luxury is a vastly different thing to different people, and you need to make sure you are defining what you think is luxury, not what you are told by others.

Luxury isn't what you think it is, or what the advertisers say. If you do something X hours X times a day/week/month, then that time, divided into the cost, is the luxury cost in real terms. So a good bed is a really good idea. Convertible sports cars are truly luxuries, and the real cost per hour of a large boat is almost beyond comprehension. Spend some time thinking about luxury and what you deserve. Be dissatisfied: commit a deadly sin (sloth included dissatisfaction, and then you are being proud enough to think you deserve something) and enjoy it.

Structured project planning has a goal, broken down into steps and segments. Partial completion is marked by milestones, and a milestone is a place for a larger reward. You don't have to have a detailed plan with exact times plugged in, and are actually encouraged not to have one. But general milestones are a good idea. Again, larger rewards are rarely as motivational as you would think, because the feedback isn't immediate. But if you reach a milestone, be nice to yourself. And rewards certainly don't have to be purchases, although something that you can see, touch, feel, or taste is going to be best. Always keep your plan open to change, to grasp new possibilities as you discover them.

Another way to frame the change process, which is a traditional psychological approach, is to ask the following questions:

> Are you ready to change; do you have the knowledge and resources to change?
>
> What is stopping you from changing? What are the barriers, internal and external?

Expect wavering relapsing, and going back to prior behavior. Just try the new behavior's again; don't dwell on "failure" and think that you're "no good" for not changing.

Again, do have some caution in using the traditional psychological literature, because as discussed before, it is focused on more socialization, not less—smoothing, not standing. More socialization is usually what people tell psychologists they want, and we all serve the customer standing before us.

> "All changes, even the most longed for, have their melancholy; for what we leave behind us is a part of ourselves; we must die to one life before we can enter another."
>
> —Anatole France

Ritual

You need rituals for yourself. A centering ritual, to achieve focus at any time and place, is a great idea. You can create your rituals yourself from the elements that feel important and happy to you. Make a haven: a special place for yourself. Tactile, smell, physical techniques reinforce the rituals.

What do you visualize when you think of a ritual? The movies have thrown many examples at us: a common one is people in cloaks, along with candles or fire, smoke, incense, and a set of actions exactly followed, accompanied by specific words.

Rituals are a set of actions with a symbolic value. These can be part of a religious service, either individually or as part of a group. Rituals can be part of what ties one to a community or identifies you as part of that community.

Rituals can happen at regular times, or as needed. The ritual can be very public or private, formal or informal. Typically, there is a clear pattern of actions, tied to thoughts and emotions.

Rituals are a formalized type of cues, which we discussed earlier when we talked about creating habits. Rituals exist for as many purposes as there are people—social needs, spiritual needs, religious observance, and the mere pleasure of the ritual. Before smoking was banned in many places (offices), smokers had a whole range of ritual motions that became part of their pleasure. The rituals probably changed when they had to stand outside in the cold twenty five feet from the door.

All societies and individuals have rituals. Groups and subgroups have different rituals, to show who is in and who is out. The rituals can be very involved, such as the ones on Halloween and Christmas, or they can be simple regular actions by friends.

We would argue that rituals do not have to be prescribed and imposed from the outside, or inherited from traditions. You can clearly create and define your own rituals, which are the most important to you.

You don't have to sacrifice animals (and we actively encourage you not to). That is taking society's model forbidden ritual hook and sinker. Actually, any kind of a sacrifice is opposite to the kind of ritual we are seeking. Sacrificial rituals give something you value to an external power. You are seeking to recover yourself and bring things of personal value together in yourself.

There are happy rituals, such as birthdays, weddings, and graduations, and sad rituals, such as funerals. The law, with courthouses and formal clothing and due process, is a ritual that takes the individual actor out of the case and substitutes the State as the actor. This is very important, because otherwise you end up with personal vendettas, which are truly a bad thing. Ritual can make you feel part of something larger or different than you feel normally. Rituals can be part of daily life: we do the same things when we wake up and go to bed, and many times in between, so rituals don't have to be tied to a formal system.

Defining your own rituals is a critical part of taking control of your life and maintaining control in times of crisis. Prince Charles was reputed to take a tattered teddy bear with him as he traveled, so that something was always home—a very important thing to do. Maintaining your happiness several levels below consciousness is very important, and it should never be neglected.

Ritualizing the act of coming to know your inner monster can be very helpful. You can define through a physical ritual in which you will let your mind wander. You can define rituals to limit the depth of the encounter, avoiding depths where the monster is still fearsome to you. While going through a ritual each day like the ones you see in the movies may be overkill-for example, keeping a cloak handy, along with candles and incense calls for considerable planning- borrowing ritual symbols has a long and honorable history. Various dictionary definitions of ritual will list of the things that have been associated with rituals, and really almost anything that people can do can be ritualized.

Making your writing a ritual is a very good idea. It can be completely under your control. Use paper you like visually, that you get pleasure from touching. Have a special notebook for this time, and a pen that you like. Make sure it feels right, the ink flows, the color is right. Simply opening up the book and hefting the pen puts you into your zone, private and comfortable.

It is especially important to have rituals when difficult things are coming out. When you are starting to understand something you have been resisting, when the ignored self is angry, it is easy to stop the process. A ritual can take control, help you through. Daily writing can show that your illusions are becoming transparent, and we all hate that. Your emotions are shouting, and you don't know what to do. Your writing/thought is showing nothing but problems; or worse, it is showing solutions that you are ignoring.

Daily writing can start to show your real feelings. Your official feelings, like your official self, are what you display. For comfort, habit, and control, part of yourself believes the official feelings, at the same time that the rest of you, lurking in the dark, growling, is rejecting them. The loss of the false self can be disorienting, traumatic. "I don't know who I am anymore," "I don't recognize myself"—these are common complaints of the logical mind crying against change. Actually, you do know who you are, but the logical mind, the censor, the sin minder, doesn't want you to know.

An important part of the strength of the inner monster is having a ritual to focus, to bring the calm that the monster and yourself brings. It can be any time, any place—a self-orienting response to find yourself. Defining those rituals for yourself to bring the monster out when you need it is helpful, otherwise surprises will freeze you like deer in the headlights. A ritual to break that freeze is going to help.

A simple ritual is to have an external symbol that you carry with you. Jewelry, a medallion, a ring, a talisman, a clothing color or combination of colors-simple things that only you know about.

Your Own Monster Can Never Turn On You, Unless You Turn On Yourself

Your inner monster can make you uncomfortable because it shows you are ignoring yourself. When you see the monster doing certain things, you start to see areas of dissatisfaction and unease that weren't aware of. When the monster is angry, listen, because part of you is trying very hard to communicate with yourself.

Remember, anytime you are tense, it is your choice, your action, your decision. You have control over your body's tension, and you can relax. Fear and tension are physical, so breathe in through your nose, out through your mouth, and get that oxygen level correct again. Move around, stretch tense muscles, and the tension will vanish. There were several quotes by Marcus Aurelius in other places in the book that deal with the concept that you choose whether to be tense or not. Again, it is hard to think outside the box and not simply react. Be careful about thinking you are supposed to deal with some idea: check your assumptions.

The monster you have chosen has chosen you. What does it look like? How do you visualize the outside? Does it have scales, is it protoplasm like a blob, does it have a hard skin like a troll? For the kind of exterior it has, what kind of environment would it live in—water, air, space, solid rock? And living in that environment, what kind of things would it run into. Why does its skin have to be like it is? Looking at the outside suddenly turns into looking at the familiar with new eyes.

One would venture that Paris Hilton's monster would be seven feet tall and tear the arms off photographers, with large troll teeth to eat the remains (as dismemberment of the paparazzi is probably a probation violation even in California).

To play with that line of thought, what kind of monster do you think other movie stars would have? What kind of monster do you think that people around you have, or are they clearly externalizing their monster already?

Monsters don't have social structures that look like human structures (at least the ones thrown at us by popular culture), so they are not fixed in the roles we see every day. Using a monster's eyes, you can look outside the leader, warrior, scribe, merchant, and laborer roles that still are the essence of the system. Think within constraints as they actually would exist, not as they are socially perceived.

Visualizing the monster is critical, because visualization is the real you in a way that words can never be. But thinking through the monster can strengthen you in several ways. You can start thinking around corners as you think what a monster's world would be. You then start to see around corners in the real world, as the thought processes transfer. You don't get the full strength of the monster if you don't understand it.

On the other hand, you don't have to do all this the first day. This is a gradual process, a voyage of self-discovery into uncharted lands. Unlike the medieval mariners, we hope there *are* monsters out there.

"If ignorant both of your enemy and yourself, you are certain to be in peril."

—Sun Tzu

Beware of rationalization. Rationalizing after the fact can make people accept anything. Rationalization can be a positive, as fighting against the impossible is pointless. Rationalizing that you can't do something because you are not spending the necessary time on that task is just flushing yourself down the toilet.

The way to guard against rationalization is to set a bottom line. You won't go past the bottom line, regardless of the circumstances. You identify what is off limits: behaviors, actions, things you won't accept, boundaries you set. Boundaries are another way of describing a bottom line.

If you focus on competition, then you are not focusing on your abilities. You lose yourself by focusing on how you are doing in comparison to others. Of course, competition exists, and you have to notice how the other people are doing. But if you read biographies of great sports heroes, they didn't focus on the competition. They focused on what they were doing and what they could do better.

"How much time he saves who does not look to see what his neighbor says or does or thinks."

—Marcus Aurelius Antoninus,
Roman emperor, A.D. 161–180

Denial is not just a river in Egypt. Denying that things went wrong or that you wanted something other than what happened chips away at yourself, by freezing your willingness to think. You know what really happened, but you hide it from yourself, you lock doors in your mind that monsters come out of later, to remind you that your inner self isn't happy. Running away from those monsters just really confuses the issue.

"Camouflage is a game we all like to play, but our secrets

are as surely revealed by what we want to seem to be as
by what we want to conceal."

—Russell Lynes

Practical Measures

With any change, any life event, it is always good to step back and
sleep on important choices. Listen to your tensions. Where are they
coming from? Are these social tensions, old habits, the official self
or the real self? The real self doesn't have a lights display to flash all
green, so you have to listen to your gut.

If you feel that things are suddenly very complex, it's probably
true. Given ten variables, combined in all the possible ways, you have
a lot of possibilities that you had ignored before. Chaos theory plays
with this—computer models can show that very simple processes become astonishingly complex. It's part of that wind blowing through
that cleared wooded lot (remember the example?). Now that the
scrub is gone, it will work out.

A useful approach to problems in life is found in the story of
Brar Rabbit and the Tar Baby. If you want to read the complete story,
do an Internet search for "Brar Rabbit"; several versions will pop
up. Essentially, Brar Rabbit is walking along and sees a tar dummy
he takes to be a person. When the dummy refuses to acknowledge
Brar Rabbit or answer his questions, he hits the dummy. First one
arm, then the other, then his legs, and finally his head are stuck to
the dummy, at which point Brar Fox, who wants to eat Brar Rabbit,
walks up.

A lot of problems in life are caused by taking on a useless battle,
which is what attacking a tar baby is. While is sounds silly to attack
a tar baby, they don't usually appear like that when you encounter
them. Commonly, they are deliberately set (with good intentions,
of course) to keep people functioning in the social environment by
keeping them uncertain, and less likely to object to things.

Remember the earlier example of the enemy that shoots the arrow that falls at your feet? Fighting a tar baby is picking that arrow
up and jabbing yourself repeatedly.

Most importantly, once you start hitting a tar baby, you just get more and more caught up in the trap. If you just leave the tar baby alone, you don't get all worked up and stuck. Can your inner monster help you see where you are attacking tar babies and wasting your time and energy? Can you step back without your inner monster and see things differently enough to know when you are hitting a tar baby?

> "The only difference between a rut and a grave is their dimensions."
>
> —Ellen Glasgow

There was a recent article on mirrors and people's responses to them in the *New York Times*[32]. Summing up the article, it is very important that people realize what they are doing. A mirror makes you recognize things about yourself, and having many mirrors is going to keep you thin better than a lock on the refrigerator.

What was interesting is that they found that physical self-reflection encouraged philosophical self-reflection, which isn't a bad thing. Along the same line is the continuing debate about weighing yourself—it is clearly better for weight control to weight yourself daily, because then you have to deal with it.

Having mirrors around the house is a good idea for several reasons. How does the mirror in your mind work to make you aware of yourself? What kind of a reflection is that mirror casting? Can you just let the reflection pop up, not trying to control it?

Society, by predefining the bets, makes it easy for you to fit in, as you don't have to think. Predefined social bets are the accepted roles and jobs pushed at all of us. If you take a predefined bet, you lose, because no one defines a bet so they lose. The level of your loss varies, but each smiling person with a proposal isn't there for your good. By defining your own bets, you have entered a far more complex world, but at least you stand a chance of winning.

---

[32] New York Times, 07/22/2008, Mirrors Don't Lie. Mislead? Oh, Yes. , Natalie Angier

"It is not necessary to change. Survival is not mandatory."

—W. Edwards Deming

Today's goal is not to convert the world. You want to feel your own gut for answers and guidance.

"Experience teaches that men are often so much governed by what they are accustomed to see and practice, that the simplest and most obvious improvements, in the most ordinary occupations, are adopted with hesitation, reluctance, and by slow gradations. Men would resist changes, so long as even a bare support could be ensured by an adherence to ancient courses, and perhaps even longer."

—Alexander Hamilton

Ninety-eight percent of life's satisfaction lies between your ears—people can have terrible things happen to them and still be happier than the idle wealthy. Who can figure?

"You can avoid having ulcers by adapting to the situation: If you fall in the mud puddle, check your pockets for fish."

—Author unknown

You have to do something five times to get comfortable at it: hanging drywall, painting a wall (not a dorm room—a wall whose appearance you care about), or anything that has several steps involved, choices, and bad results from many of those choices. Don't quit after the first muddled attempt. It is that muddling that is the learning experience. Again, new habits, not changing old ones.

If you want to learn, explore the thought in different senses, in different places. You need to experience the new in multiple ways for it to start sinking in for change. It is important, although it sounds basic, to get up, move around, and get the brain in gear. The traditional view that you should sit very still while the brain works, like many traditional views, could hardly be more wrong. The whole body is involved with the brain working, and the research shows there is more creativity and thought when the body moves. Don't try mental gymnastics while trying to cross New York streets against the light—anything can be taken too far—but be more like a child and move around.

As we have said several times, remember that externalization is generally a response to socialization, and as an actor in a morality play fed to you. Your inner unrecognized frustrations and angers acting out that play can destroy you. Remember, society has people with guns who have bought into the system as it is, so unless you are Godzilla, don't push it. Patrick Henry, the American Patriot, said "Give me liberty or give me death," but he said it in the colonies; he didn't travel to London to make the announcement, because they would have given him death. Don't be stupid.

The 2004 tsunami that killed so many people shows the danger of socialization. People stood at the edge of the water, and the water receded. They looked at each other, no one panicked, and they walked out, following the water, until it *really* came back in. The correct response was to run like hell the other way, but as no one else near them did, they didn't. There are many tsunamis in your personal, financial, and economic world that are not clearly dangerous at first. You have to think, because the talking heads don't see it, and if they did, they wouldn't tell you anyway.

Things to Remember While Feeding

You want your monster to protect you. Monsters are very good at the rough stuff—and the rough stuff inside is tougher than the stuff outside.

Don't restrict yourself to scarcity thinking—that you have only so much luck and don't want to seek something because you are using all your luck. Focus yourself on something, and luck will pop up. Do what you don't care about, and all you find is bad luck.

Your monster takes you to the places you need to be. These are places you have been ignoring, because it seems to be not allowed or seems likely to cause problems, even though you are fighting through many problems caused by not facing the issues.

Your inner monster is critical to yourself—it *is* you, all the "you" that the village ethics doesn't need. You need to feed your monster so that you are fully alive.

Your monster gives you strength and power to stand alone when the crowd is against you, when things are changing and others refuse to recognize it.

Using your monster isn't weakness; living through your social self is weakness.

Chapter 19. Active Meditation and Active Peace

Active Meditation

Active meditation is opening to your monster. It is the active mental process of finding yourself. You are touching on your emotions, especially your hidden emotions. You are feeling and experimenting with anger, envy, greed, lust, pride—all the forbidden things. You are actively thinking through what is good for you, what is damaging to you, the freight loaded on by society with those words so that you follow the their line. You are clarifying your internal self, feeling and seeing where you are. You are letting the non-verbal portions of your mind come out and play.

Traditional meditation, a process of clearing your mind to the empty void, to become one with yourself, is actually the opposite process of finding your monster. Traditional meditation wanted to escape from yourself, finding comfort in the disappearance of self into the greater something. Traditional meditation seeks the non-verbal part, the feelings, and hopes that those will come to you as you clear your mind into a void.

Active meditation is clearing out the social rules that keep you confused and frustrated. You want to find yourself, the dark, the powerful parts of yourself, and bring those into your daily life. With traditional meditation, you have to avoid the noise and confusion. Back into the noise and confusion, the peace of meditation vanishes, and you have to use a borrowed ritual to get it back.

As you are actively meditating, can you feel the monster with your vision, taste, touch, hearing, and smell? Can you think about each in different ways? Can you combine them into something unexpected? We learn by using our senses, which is why reading in the library is often nap time. The more senses you use, the more you combine them, the more you will grow. Imagine seeing different wavelengths, touching with different sensors, tasting ... well, what do monsters eat?

If you think that imagining seeing in different wavelengths is unrealistic, within a very few years, there will be replacement eyes for people who are blind. What wavelengths could a mechanical replacement eye pick up? The answer is any wavelength that can be caught by the equipment. So that change is coming quickly.

What emotions do you think a monster would have? Are there emotions that are like different visual wavelengths? Are they limited to feeling only what humans feel? This is really opening your mind to the new.

Life actually is the beach. The beach is constant change: waves, wind, clouds, sun moving, people coming and going, birds flying, and remembering to make sure you are not burning in the sun. You don't hold the beach still in your mind; it is the motion and change that is the experience. It is no different in life, except that the waves of life take longer to break and reform. We are lulled by our perceptions of time and suddenly awake when the rip tide starts pulling at us.

Again, because this is really different, meditation—clearing your mind to become one with the universe, or something—is the opposite process of finding your monster. Active meditation, however, is the mental process of finding yourself through opening up to the forbidden parts of yourself. With traditional meditation, you were to escape from yourself, finding comfort in the disappearance of self into the void. Thus you see your insignificance, and you can relax (or something like that). Active meditation wants you to come to yourself, the dark, the power parts of yourself, and bring those into your daily life. You want to feel how important you are, because you are all you've got.

In Monty Python's *The Meaning of Life*, a man walks into a house, pulls out a scalpel, and takes out the husband's liver, without anesthesia, a surprise to the donor. The donor card said "in the event of death," so the man extracting the liver says, "No one who has ever had their liver taken out by us has survived." There was evidently some confusion about the terms, which is why you shouldn't assume definitions. The man then talks the wife into donating her liver, as the husband lies in the room screaming, slowly dying. You will notice the man collecting livers didn't donate his liver, and all the nonsense about the stars being big and you being small didn't change his focus, so why should you fall for it? How many times in your life did a person ask you to make a difficult choice and benefit from it, even though he would not make this choice himself?

In your active meditation, try a democracy in your mind, listening to diverse voices. A dictatorship is listening to only one view, and the view you have been told is not even your own. Your inner monster gives you different viewpoints. Socialization, based on habit and frozen behaviors, diminishes and destroys the person. Your monster can handle the others who throw the tricks and traps at you.

As you relax and experiment with monsters, do you find one that suddenly makes you relax? Does your core just relax, and do you involuntarily take a deep, relaxed breath when you visualize it? That discovery can't be forced; it just comes out of the side of your mind. Feel that relaxation—the muscles of your chest, abdominals, and hips.

Relaxed means that your body moves around, and you look around. You notice things that you just looked past before. Colors are brighter, sounds more important. Your perception of time changes. Don't back away from that feeling; don't just slip into the official focus that is habit.

We would venture you would not have been comfortable with such a visual before reading this. Perhaps it was a monster you were running from? That is the visual you want to work with: when you deeply physically relax, you have hit gold. Pull that monster into your vision. Feel it flowing through you, giving you strength. You need that visual to meditate with, to be able to pull to you when things are intense.

Discovery is of course the finding the new. The more you feel yourself to be on terra incognita, the more certain you can be that you are making progress, even though it isn't always a comfortable feeling.

Discovering the new, discovering yourself, begins in darkness. There may be flashes of light, sudden points where you "get it," but bright ideas have a gestation period that is interior, murky, and necessary. Ideas grow like life, arising from the muck, pushing up through the soil. Your ideas change and develop in drips and drops. No one makes a full-blown discovery, all perfect and glowing. Even when you discover your path, it takes weeding and experimenting.

Don't push and pull on your ideas. Don't force them into complete and final outlines. You jot things and you move things, you push things to the side and see how they fit later. This isn't a homework assignment, with clear parameters and exact source material to review. You let the ideas grow organically, with twists and turns and blossoms where you didn't expect any.

Remember, life is like a puzzle, with no picture of the finished puzzle to works towards, with pieces that don't seem to be related, given to you over time. Sometimes one doesn't even see the pieces as they are given. Can you put the puzzle together yourself for your life, or will you let others give you their solved puzzle, which meets their needs?

You want to surrender to the creation process; you can't control it. When you have a clear goal, then you can create a formal plan, but formal plans for creation don't work anywhere, to tell the truth. The statistics on project management failure, where there is a clear physical creation goal with known supplies and resources, are astonishingly high. You can't expect control and a clear plan where you are letting the monster find you, letting your actual self gradually emerge.

Enjoy the mystery at the heart of growth and creativity. Enjoy the surprise when new things pop up. Ideas need to rise, just like bread—bang on them too early and they sink. Let your ideas form in a dark cave in your mind, building up like stalactites and stalagmites. Then, when you flash a light on them, they will reflect back like the treasure cave of Ali Baba and the Forty Thieves: all you had to say was "Open sesame."

Growth is different from productivity. Productivity is the creation of X under a firm set of rules. Growth is something new, and it is generally far more productive than non-growth, but in a different way.

Nothing is fixed. Nothing is safe. Nothing is really controllable. You fool yourself if you believe differently and don't take that into account. So trust the dark parts of your mind, gently mulling ideas as they come to you instead of churning down a track. If you run down a track, you know exactly what distance you cover, but it's pretty much the same track every day. If you run through the woods, by the river, it's a different experience each day—be open to those experiences.

Active meditation accepts that you are organic, emotional, selfish, and focused on yourself. Remember Clint Eastwood's classic line: "A man has to know his limitations." We all have limits, and you will enjoy yourself more as yourself, not as a picture you were handed and try to live up to.

Active meditation is going to tell you that you are different than you thought. Sometimes we just change. Horror of horrors, one of the authors doesn't seem as obsessed with chocolate as he used to be. Shifts in taste and perception frequently happen as you shift identity. A bright light that something healthy is afoot is the impulse to weed out, sort through, and discard old stuff. Those old clothes, papers, and belongings that we accumulate represent the past.

Do you ever wonder why you work yourself to death for certain furnishings, only to toss them five years later? It makes one decide to spend more on experience, which is easier to pack and take along with one. By tossing out the old and unworkable, we make way for the new and suitable

So be open to the search and discard impulse seizing you. There are two things going on: the new you is celebrating and growing, and the old you is leaving and sad. Change happens. There will be an odd mix of emotions, and sometimes it's hard to determine what to do. If you have an image in your mind of what you want, then you should do that. It's as true for a hot fudge sundae as it is for your new life plan. If you compromise on the sundae and get an ice cream bar, inside you will pout, and you will get the sundae very soon anyhow.

In a sense, you are cleaning. In the cleaning, you see yourself more clearly in the mirror in your mind. You can see shapes, not the blurs or hazes that you quickly walked by before. Your inner self, your actual self, is there, and your official self is now haze.

Active medication is a time to fill yourself with images. You need time to process the images that are floating around and let the mind make connections, which you need to listen to. Whether you want to consider this mining for treasure, letting your well of creativity fill up, planting seeds in your mind, or any combination of metaphors you want, let it happen.

Mystery is a critical part of all creativity, spiritual feelings, emotional growth, and religion. The unknown is out there, and suddenly you understand, feel a part of it. Bring that mystery into your life, your goals—you don't always have to buy it premade and processed. Finding and accepting your inner monster is a step toward embracing the forbidden, a step toward being a real person, not a list of accepted behaviors. This is you working with you: no shame, no anxiety.

Active meditation should be practiced daily. You want to practice reaching for strength at various times and places. Trying only when you absolutely need it isn't the best approach.

Dynamic, Active, Functioning Peace

Emotional peace is one of those things you want most when you don't have it. Fixating on wanting peace can almost drive you crazy by itself. The Beatles song "So Tired" is a place you don't want to be.

> "If you are pained by external things, it is not they that disturb you, but your own judgment of them. And it is in your power to wipe out that judgment now."
>
> —Marcus Aurelius Antoninus,
> Roman emperor, A.D. 161–180

It is absolutely key to remember that fear is physically seated. Various combinations of muscle reactions, coupled with lack of oxygen, are the main cause of fear and panic. Simple things: breathing in through nose, out through the mouth, can bring calm suddenly.

As you grow to your inner monster, and the inner monsters you feared become comfortable, it is easier to see how fear is just physical. Everyone has certain muscle feelings they are afraid of. Anxiety, panic, fear: we all jump when we hit that spot, just like when the dentist wanders onto a live nerve with his drill.

Once you are comfortable with your monster, you can play with those feelings you were afraid of. It is absolute amazing: something

194

that used to make you just stop dead and freeze, you can now feel and then release, feel and release. You don't need whatever borrowed ritual you used to use to control or avoid that feeling. Hit that feeling, and then just focus on your monster visualization. The feeling vanishes. Go back, get the feeling going again; play with the receptors, the habit cues for that response. Go to your monster, back and forth.

It's almost scary that you can do it. It feels as if it should be forbidden, because we are taught that these fears have such power. We are taught that the only way around your fears is a society ritual you have to pay for. Suddenly being able to pull your own strings is amazing—and no expensive drugs are required. The limiting, official self—the parasite that pulls your energy into useless activity—vanishes.

Passive peace is too often a control mechanism. Peaceful in a quiet room is one thing, but when the world pops up again, that peace is gone. You have to follow the rented social ritual to achieve peace again. Active peace is peace in the middle of the chaos.

We want peace after being beaten on to regain our bearings. A physical beating is usually easier to recover from than the emotional beatings. Emotional beatings worm their way in and twist and turn in our guts if we don't do something to get them out.

Criticism is a type of a beating. Adults stand there, smiling and nodding, taking others' "advice." But emotionally we are four years old inside, and we are furious and hurt.

When you have been criticized, do this:

a. Remember, you have to inflict this beating inside you. You have to pick up the arrow and jab yourself in the chest. If you don't, the rejection floats away into the past.

b. Think the criticism all the way through and get it over with. If there is anything useful, make some notes for next time. You paid for this experience; you might as well get something useful out of it.

c. Do something for yourself—be kind to yourself. The very last thing you want to do is to punish yourself.

d. Mistakes are necessary—if you were perfect, your position in the celestial order would be much higher, and your responsibilities much higher. As pointed out earlier, moving the goal posts so that something looks right is how the world works. Don't get trapped in perfectionism.

e. Get back to work—do something. You will feel better about yourself doing something, and the doing will drive out the negative thoughts, the logical mind shouting that were you never any good. *Do* and move forward.

This isn't new advice, by the way. Slightly rephrasing the last quote:

> "If you are distressed by anything external, the pain is not due to the thing itself, but to your estimate of it; and this you have the power to revoke at any moment."
>
> —Marcus Aurelius Antoninus,
> Roman emperor, A.D. 161–180

Active peace comes from active meditation. It comes from reaching into your actual self and feeling comfortable. It comes from your inner monster filling you, focusing your efforts, pushing off the socialization nonsense so you can exist now and move through the problem. If you are facing a real problem at the same time working through the "I think that they think that I think that they think…" routine, you are going to lose focus of the real problem and just stew.

Re-read the "Wrath/Anger" section in "Vices," and think about anger. Bring your rage and envy into you; embrace your sins to strengthen you. Be proud of what you are, not false proud of what you want to be.

Chapter 20: Individualism, Character, and Your Inner Monster

In the early days of the country, the United States believed in the power of the individual. A person could be what they wanted, achieve what they wanted, rise beyond the frozen social structure of Europe and the old world. Of course it wasn't exactly like that, but people could make better lives for themselves than the lives they would have been frozen into in the cultures they came from.

Ralph Waldo Emerson and Henry David Thoreau were respected American writers who believed in the importance of the individual. They were required reading when I was in high school and college, although we're not sure they are favored by the educational establishment at present.

> "I went to the woods because I wished to live deliberately, to front only the essential facts of life, and see if I could not learn what it had to teach, and not, when I came to die, discover that I had not lived."
>
> —Henry David Thoreau, 1854

Their books are still enjoyable and inspiring, and while they were lighter in tone than the themes in this book, their message on the importance of the individual and self-determination is certainly monstrous in today's social order.

The social consensus as to the innate value of individualism has ebbed and flowed over time. The 1950s were generally considered a time of high conformity, with the later 1960s and early 1970s focusing more on individual freedoms and options.

At some point in the last twenty years, the individual seems to have become a bad thing. Teamwork is the mantra at work. Cooperation is what is taught in schools and seminars. Individuals became the loner in the house that they find bodies in, the person who doesn't get along at work. Individuals are concerned with things like their life and balance, rather than external shows and corporate results.

The focus of the TV talk shows, and the books they promote, are to bring you into the group, not be the individual who stands out. You can be the "individual" that the group respects for the embodiment of group virtues, but not the individual who annoys people. So now we live in a subdivision that dictates the color, design, and options for your complete exterior, down to your mailbox and yard edging, and woe to those who fall outside. The grown-up schoolyard bully, the attorney on retainer, is always ready to pounce as paid.

Perhaps TV is part of the change. Individuals don't show well on TV, as it is a social medium, people talking to each other. What mass market show today isn't a group of people in front of an audience, the embodiment of group think and consensus?

School, from kindergarten through twelfth grade, is a training ground for the system—you do what you are told, when you are told, and how you are told. Socialization is important—everyone has to agree on certain things. The economic system doesn't work if people can't read, write, and perform certain mathematical tasks. As is clear to everyone, our present school system was designed for an industrial system, to turn haphazard agricultural labor's partially structured behavior into tight time-oriented channels.

Individuals can't be controlled by the group. Individuals don't do what, when, and how they are told. Individuals may want more education, more challenges, which are unfair to those with lesser abilities. Individuals may even question the abilities of some of the teachers, the ultimate sin.

> The essence of individualism is to choose the standards one aspires to. One may choose majority standards, minority standards, original standards, or no standards at all. Again, the actual choice does not prove individualist reasoning—one must look to the reasoning itself. Thus the only defining quality of an individualist is that she uses a personal command of logical principles to give all options a fair and equal evaluation before making a decision or conclusion. This process should certainly include evaluation of existing standards widely held. The individualist

relies on her own judgment only to the extent that, after much evaluation, she finds it objectively superior to that of another.[33]

Subtlety seems to have been lost on our ancestors. They simply killed people who annoyed them. People who have stood out, people who challenged or fought the social system, have been weeded out over the past five thousand years. In agrarian society, the abilities needed were few, the work was awful, and the discipline intense—killing a few to keep the others in line cost nothing, and it could be considered a net savings in calories. We are fortunate now that individualism doesn't have those threats to face.

Character is determined at the individual level. You don't get to borrow character from the group identity; it is you as an individual, which only you can earn. Moral character is a set of qualities that one person has in different proportions than other people. The qualities are defined in different ways, and certainly can be socially slanted, but generally they include the concepts of integrity, courage, honesty, and fortitude.

> "Character, in the long run, is the decisive factor in the life of an individual and of nations alike."
>
> —Theodore Roosevelt

There has been much hand wringing about ethics in today's world: Arthur Andersen, the respected accounting firm, went off a cliff because of failure of vision at the top. There have been, and will continue to be, massive financial frauds and accounting violations, company failures and collapses. In those situations, many in the companies involved knew what was happening. Some complained, but most shut up and did their jobs, because the social environment said to shut up. The finest degrees, distinguished work histories and backgrounds, all thrown away because they couldn't face what they knew in their heart, and it eventually ate them.

---

[33] Wikipedia, "Individualism," http://en.wikipedia.org/wiki/Individualism.

Social character, stripped of the elegant wording, is doing graciously what you are beaten into doing, and thanking your oppressors for it. That is what the monster wants you to see past and understand.

So here we are, focusing on your inner monster, and we're claiming character points for the monster? The book has focused on how people trick and trap you with invalid social makers. Your goal in feeding your inner monster is to understand and be yourself, which means you must then do the right things for yourself. The monster gives you strength to act and to focus on what you see as right, which is character, the essence of individualism.

Your monster, by making you see differently, defines and focuses your character. Some of the social virtues are absolutely necessary for the group to continue, and understanding those is absolutely rational. Your monster likes to eat. Some of the vices are actually dangerous to you, and your monster prefers a continued existence. Determining what has to be done and what should be avoided, and acting on those choices, is truly personal character.

> "To dare to live alone is the rarest courage; since there are many who had rather meet their bitterest enemy in the field, than their own hearts in their closet."
>
> —Charles Caleb Colton, Lacon, 1825

Chapter 21: Discovery and Growth

Now it's time to work with what you have discovered. Your writing, thinking, reading, and the time you've made for yourself have opened you to new thinking. Growth is going back to the monster when you want to—doing it gradually, trying something small every day. It's a good idea to read back through different parts of the book occasionally, to jog some new thoughts or break through to another track.

> "Far better to dare mighty things, to win glorious triumphs, even though checkered by failure, than to take rank with those poor spirits who neither enjoy much nor suffer much, because they live in the grey twilight that knows not victory, nor defeat."
>
> —President Theodore Roosevelt, 1899

If there is something bothering you, remember you had to let it in to bother you. Like vampires, problems have to stop at your threshold and wait to be invited inside. You don't have to invite them inside. You have a choice.

A key point of this book is that if you accept what is defined as the dark, which is life, you will function far better and not be self-destructive (in the true sense of the term).

The critical action you have to do is to take at least one small step every day. Don't decide to change your life completely in one day. Take the small steps. Set a timer and do something for fifteen minutes. The changes will come from inside, naturally. Forced change from the outside doesn't work. Mentally taking that step to accept and seek your inner monster is a key decision. Accepting that you are "good" and society is "bad" is an enormous mental change that is going to take some time to implement.

This book, as you have noticed by getting this far, has a dark, intense edge. It doesn't put happy faces on monsters or the world, because we have no desire to fool you. The world isn't fooled, and it doesn't even care, really. This isn't *Foster's Home for Imaginary Friends* (a cartoon show on the The Cartoon Chanel, which we happen to like a lot, by the way). This is a serious attempt to do some inside strengthening and fitness, some hardening, not polite conversation.

What if you could revitalize your DNA? What if your body could regenerate? It will happen eventually, and quite likely pretty soon. What about the Transformers from the cartoons and movies: what will happen when some body functions are turned into steel, and we have replaceable parts? Then will you be a monster. What would you think then about daily life, and what would be important to you if you could live for a thousand years?

The real issue will be when the wealthy can live much longer, imposing their control and frozen beliefs over generations. Too often, change occurs in the real world simply when the prior generation dies out. What if Lenin were still alive? Worse yet, Stalin?

The medical research that will lead to these changes is being done in small pieces all over the world. The usual human response—"We won't allow it"—fortunately or unfortunately, won't happen, because these changes are too widespread and too important to be restricted. If your soldiers could regenerate body parts, if they had mechanical devices to encase them, that research will continue, because you can't let the other side get there first.

You can't force opportunity. Your emotional need for results is different from real opportunity. Build strength, and then you will see opportunity.

> "Invincibility lies in oneself. Vincibility lies in the enemy... Thus the skilled can make themselves invincible. They cannot cause the enemy's vincibility. Thus it is said, "Victory can be known. It cannot be made."[34]

As discussed before, the skills and mindset you need will change as you pass through new stages. With a job, it's easier to see when things have changed. In life, sometimes the hardest part is to notice that things have changed, and to change focus.

---

[34] Sut-Tzu, The Art of Warfare, (The Modern Library, 2000) pp 13, Form

"What lies behind us and what lies before us are small matters compared to what lies within us."

—Ralph Waldo Emerson

There will be happy times coming, but there will be hard times. There will be widespread sicknesses, economic disruption, and disasters to face. There will be car accidents, house floods, and children doing poorly in school and life. Do you have the energy to carry through? You can't count on help from others; you have to do it with inside power. When the power lines are down, you have to be your generator.

Change in this world doesn't always blow a trumpet when it comes. As Horatio said in *Hamlet*,

A mote it is to trouble the mind's eye.

In the most high and palmy state of Rome.

A little ere the mighiest Julius fell.

The graves stood tenantless and the sheeted dead

Did squeak and gibber in the Roman streets;
As stars with trains of fire, and dews of blood,
Disasters in the sun; and the moist star.[35]

You have to keep your eyes open. Don't live this quote:

"I change my opinions often, but not my way of thinking."

—Mason Cooley

Your inner monster is here to bring new thinking to your life. You have to protect yourself. If you see a wave coming, move out

---

[35] William Shakespeare, Hamlet, act 1, scene 1.

of the way. If you are standing at the edge of the ocean, and the water suddenly recedes – run like hell. Don't look at the other people on the beach and use their reactions to judge the extent of the danger. Don't limit the example to the water, because there are lots of situations in life where you can make a more informed decision about action that the people standing next to you. Don't limit your behavior to their lesser expertise.

> "In the province of the mind, what one believes to be true either is true or becomes true."
>
> —John Lilly

In Conclusion

Monty Python has a wonderful sketch, where a person accused of a crime goes into a soliloquy about the importance of freedom. It is in the "How to Recognize Different Types of Tress from Quote a Long Way Away" program, and unfortunately they refused to grant permission to use the quote. In essence, it eloquently praised freedom in wonderful eighteenth century phrases. (It's probably better to watch it on TV, as the actors' intonation makes the speech.) After this wonderful speech, the judge tells the defendant that it's only a parking offense, and so all the wonderful words were not necessary.

That is society dismissing your real concerns: don't buy that it's just a parking offence—they know better.

> "It is true that liberty is precious; so precious that it must be carefully rationed."
>
> —Vladimir Ilyich Lenin

Tell Yourself of the Darkness Within

Now tell yourself of the darkness within: how is it different from the inner darkness you saw when you started the book?

Printed in the United States
148691LV00003B/4/P